THE SILVERSMITH'S ART

MADE IN BRITAIN TODAY

Inside cover key:

Chasing	*Engraving*	*Shaping*
Detail from *Deluge Dish* by Miriam Hanid	Detail from *Colour Junction* by Jane Short	Detail from *Pine Cone* by Junko Mori
Detail from *Diamond Jubilee Dish* by Rod Kelly	Detail from *Millennium Casket* by Malcolm Appleby	Detail from *Vase* by William Lee
Detail from *Bowl* by Michael Lloyd	Detail from *Vase* by Angus McFadyen	Detail from *Negative Bowl* by Ane Christensen

D1492748

THE SILVERSMITH'S ART

MADE IN BRITAIN TODAY

The 21st Century Silver Collection of the
Worshipful Company of Goldsmiths

The Goldsmiths' Company
London MMXV

The GOLDSMITHS' Company

Published in the UK by The Goldsmiths' Company,
for the exhibition at the National Museums
Scotland, Edinburgh, from 18 September 2015
to 4 January 2016 with financial support from
The Goldsmiths' Company Charity and a
financial contribution from Bonhams Edinburgh
and London.

Catalogue by Rosemary Ransome Wallis

ISBN 978 0 907814 33 7

Exhibition works photographed
by Clarissa Bruce and Richard Valencia
Designed and typeset in Kingfisher by Dalrymple
Printed in Belgium by Albe De Coker

Cover: details from *Tectonic Beakers I & II*, 2014
silver by Malcolm Appleby and enamel
by Jane Short.

Frontispiece: detail from Theresa Nguyen
'Parissa' Centrepiece, 2009

Bonhams

CONTENTS

7 Preface

8 The Worshipful Company of Goldsmiths

11 Studio Silver in the 21st Century: its development and definition

19 CATALOGUE

203 Hallmarking

204 The UK Assay Offices

205 Directory of Sponsors' Marks

Malcolm Appleby 20
Alex Brogden 24
Clive Burr 27
Jocelyn Burton 30
Julie Chamberlain 32
Ane Christensen 33
David Clarke 36
Kevin Coates 38
Rosamond Conway 40
Angela Cork 42
Rebecca de Quin 48
Stuart Devlin 53
Lexi Dick 56
Sidsel Dorph-Jensen 58
Ndidi Ekubia 60
Richard Fox 62
Kevin Grey 64
Miriam Hanid 65
Rauni Higson 70
Kathryn Hinton 76
Adrian Hope 78
Kyosun Jung 82
Petya Kapralova 84
Rod Kelly 86
Chris Knight 92
William (Sang-Hyeob) Lee 94
Nan Nan Liu 100
Michael Lloyd 101
Esther Lord 106
Anna Lorenz 110
Olivia Lowe 112
Frances Loyen 113
Grant Macdonald 114

Grant McCaig 116
Alistair McCallum 118
Sheila McDonald 122
Angus McFadyen 126
Wayne Meeten 130
Hector Miller 132
Junko Mori 134
Theresa Nguyen 138
Cóilín O'Dubhghaill 142
Shannon O'Neill 145
Steven Ottewill 148
Carl Padgham & Andrew Putland 150
Christopher Perry 153
Don Porritt 154
Alex Ramsay 155
Clare Ransom 156
Alexandra Raphael 158
Pamela Rawnsley 160
Fred Rich 164
Linda Robertson 165
Michael Rowe 168
Toby Russell 170
Jane Short 172
Mary Ann Simmons 180
Hiroshi Suzuki 182
Lucian Taylor 186
Simone Ten Hompel 188
Hazel Thorn 190
Adi Toch 193
Keith Tyssen 196
Max Warren 198
Yusuke Yamamoto 200

Detail of 'Negative' Bowl by Ane Christensen

A livery dinner at Goldsmiths' Hall with modern silver buffet plate display, 2015

generally towards primary, secondary and further education, particularly in the world of science. For instance, the Company funds a Chair of Material Science at Cambridge University.

Internationally recognised, the Goldsmiths' Company has one of the finest collections of silver made in Britain, numbering some 8,000 examples from 1350 to the present day. The special character of the collection, which divides into groups: antique silver, domestic silver, contemporary silver, jewellery and art medals, is that all the items are used either for their original purpose, or for display in exhibitions, or to inspire outside contemporary patronage of living craftsmen.

Recent major modern silver commissions by outside patrons include ecclesiastical silver for Lichfield Cathedral, for the Dio Padre Misericordioso, Rome and for York Minster; all dining silver for the Silver Trust at No.10 Downing Street; The Rabinovitch Collection at the Victoria and Albert Museum; and the John Keatley Trust and The Makower Trust, which provide modern silver for National Museums.

These commissions emphasise the Goldsmiths' Company's own deliberate pioneering patronage, which has enhanced creative vitality of design and craftsmanship in silver throughout the 20th century and continues today in the 21st century.

STUDIO SILVER IN THE 21st CENTURY: ITS DEVELOPMENT & DEFINITION

What is the value of a silver beaker today by the artist silversmith Michael Lloyd? Is it the material of silver? Is it the skilful hand-chasing of the imagery or is it his creative artistry?

To answer these questions an understanding of how the perception of silver, its value and use, has changed over the last 200 years needs to be explored.

BACKGROUND

In 19th century Britain, with its intense industrialisation, a distinction between the fine arts and the applied arts was forcefully formulated. Machinery, the aid to production, had been playing an increasingly important part in the manufacture of silver since the latter part of the 18th century. Smaller silver workshops were absorbed into larger businesses. As a result large scale companies in the 19th century employed designers to express the national fashion of the day. For example, the royal retail firm, Rundell, Bridge and Rundell (1797–1843) employed the designer, William Theed, sculptor, and on his death employed another sculptor, John Flaxman. Their designs, and design details, were then made up by the silversmithing workshops of Paul Storr and the partnership of Benjamin Smith & Digby Scott, considered then the best craftsmen in London, who between them produced a vast amount of silver: 10,000 ounces a month. The prosperity of Rundell, Bridge and Rundell was partly due to the royal patronage of the flamboyant King George IV, partly due to the firm's position as manufacturer and retailer, with agents in the Middle and Far East and in South America, and partly due to

the firm's considerable stock of new and old silver at its shop, The Golden Salmon, 32 Ludgate Hill, London.

Today, the work of Rundell, Bridge and Rundell is highly regarded and fetches substantial prices in auctions of antique silver. However, by the end of the 19th century there was a plethora of silver manufacturing companies in London, Birmingham, Sheffield and Chester, making wares to meet the national social demand for silver and silver plate for dining and ceremonial use. The advertisements for James Dixon & Sons, Sheffield in 1864, for example, describe the company as 'Merchants and Manufacturers of Presentation Plate, Silver and Silver-Plated Goods, Nickel Silver and Electro-Plated Nickel Silver. Spoons and Forks, Desserts Etc.'

This manufacturing ethos for silver mass production lasted well into the 20th century. In 1926 the Clerk of the Goldsmiths' Company, George Hughes, published *The Plate of The Worshipful Company of Goldsmiths* saying 'This work taught me more about silver and its tradition than anything... The idea of the old craft guild sponsoring a revival gradually took shape. There was a need for a revival; the industry was depressed and un-enterprising. Apart from the work of the artist craftsman...'

The reaction against the conservative Edwardian delight in the splendour of Historic Revivalist styles was an avant-garde attitude in cultural circles of society. There was a yearning for the honesty of craftsmanship. 'As a condition of life, production by machine is altogether an evil'. This was the view of the social reformer, William Morris, who had begun his own firm in 1861 dedicated to bringing art and craftsmanship to all objects of everyday life. His view, in turn, inspired, at

above: Pair of coasters, 1810, by Benjamin and James Smith for Rundell, Bridge and Rundell

opposite: Beaker, 2006 by Michael Lloyd

Crumb Scoop, c.1900, electroplate

Exhibition poster, 1938

Grant Macdonald, designer silversmith's, workshop

An employee using Computer Aided Design

the beginning of the 20th century the English Arts and Crafts Movement, whose ideals of craftsmanship – although developed – have remained a strength in silver design throughout the 20th and 21st centuries.

THE GOLDSMITHS' COMPANY'S MODERN SILVER COLLECTION

Faced with a very loosely constituted silver trade, the Goldsmiths' Company decided in 1926 to begin a collection of modern silver, to improve the design and craftsmanship in the precious metals. In addition, by naming the individual silversmiths acquired, the Company created collectability of their work. This initiative focused the Company's effectiveness, as it still does today, as the principal patron of the craft.

The Modern Silver Collection, dating from 1926–2015 numbers 944 items. Consistently over this period of 80 years up to 12 items of modern silver have been added annually, either by purchase or commission. The Collection overall provides a comprehensive picture of the development of modern silver, demonstrating innovative design and dexterity of craftsmanship at the highest level, as well as providing an insight into the Company's informed patronage. Over the years aspects of the Modern Silver Collection have been displayed in numerous exhibitions, both in Britain and overseas, as part of the Company's support of the silver craft. Catalogues and books have recorded the Collection and individual silversmiths. Students, having seen the Collection, have been inspired to follow silversmithing as a career.

Hand chasing

Rapid prototype resin model

Michael Lloyd, artist silversmith

Rauni Higson, artist silversmith

Outside patrons too have been inspired by the Collection to commission new work from living silversmiths. Today, Britain leads the world in contemporary silver design, and at the centre of this modern movement is the heartbeat of the Worshipful Company of Goldsmiths.

COMPOSITION OF THE COLLECTION 2000–2015

There are only a few large scale reproduction silver companies left in Britain. Most outsource the manufacture of their silverware to the Far East to make up traditional styles, such as King's pattern cutlery, Queen Anne coffee pots and Chippendale pie crust salvers. Innovative production designs today are now focused on several established designer silversmiths workshops. These small companies cater for the bespoke market in the United Kingdom, the Middle East and Russia, as well as for contemporary retail markets. There are seven designer silversmiths represented in the 21st century collection; leading names include Richard Fox, Grant Macdonald, Clive Burr and Steven Ottewill. These designer silversmiths are distinguished from artist silversmiths in that they acknowledge the restraint of working with a client's specification for bespoke pieces and quantity orders. To achieve such contemporary designs, quality traditional craftsmanship is combined with the latest engineering and technological aids, their workshops employing a number of skilled craftsman and ancillary staff. This enables the designer silversmiths' companies to meet satisfactory pricing, as well as producing a quality product which bears the respected brand of the chosen designer silversmith's workshop.

The other 59 artist silversmiths represented in the Collection, 2000–2015, are at the centre of the debate about the arts today, not only about the distinction between the fine arts and applied arts, but about the distinction between art and craft.

Can silversmithing be regarded as an art form in its own right, akin to sculpture? No such distinction existed in the 16th century: Botticelli was apprenticed to a goldsmith to learn the discipline of draughtsmanship. So how is an artist defined – concept to execution? An artist silversmith has personal control of every aspect of the creative process, combining concept, design and most of the execution in a single pair of hands. There is no restraint, just as there is no restraint for artists who paint, or sculptors who sculpt. As a result these artist silversmiths have a distinctive, recognisable singularity, an individuality, which is expressed in a personal, non-verbal language in the medium of silver, responding to a patron's commission, or realising a different concept. Silver is seen by the artist silversmith as a medium for self-expression, and a means of communicating that expression. There is an empathy with the material and the subject matter. Each work is a one-off and cannot be repeated exactly.

Design drawing for Kedleston Beaker by Theresa Nguyen

Theresa Nguyen, artist silversmith

THE SKILFUL USE OF SILVERSMITHING HAND-TECHNIQUES IN CONTEMPORARY SILVER

Like musical composers, artist silversmiths today create unique compositions using techniques as instruments of silversmithing. Artist silversmiths work with their material intuitively, exploring the possibilities of silver by adapting traditional techniques innovatively to produce their original designs. Enamel colours can accentuate the expressive qualities of a composition; contradictions and harmonies of form can provoke a dialogue of ideas in the observer. The viewer's expectation is changed by reconfiguration and redefining of surfaces and structures made in silver. This expert working of silver forms a non-verbal language for all to interpret and contemplate.

The most traditional silversmithing technique of all is hand-raising. Initially using a hammer, and a steel stake, secured in a tree trunk, a sturdy bench, or a leg vice, the silver sheet is compressed over the stake by the hammer's blows. The silver is then annealed (softened) to allow further forming. Hand-planishing, the final hammering operation, smoothes the silver surface by applying accurately aimed hammer blows. The silver can then be filed and prepared for polishing.

The 'Moon' Vase, 2010, by William Lee is a large scale example of hand raising from a single sheet of silver.

The oldest known silversmithing technique is hand-forging, which simply uses a hammer and anvil. It is commonly used to make handmade spoons but Junko Mori uses this technique to make her highly original 'Pine Cone', 2007.

Other traditional techniques include sinking to make a tray, illustrated by Rauni Higson's 'Iris' Salver, 2009; seaming and fabricating sheet silver over formers, such as the seemingly simple 'Two Streams' Vinaigrette, 2001, by Linda Robertson; caulking an edge to a beaker such as Beaker, 2014, by Ndidi Ekubia; piercing to cut out a design, as can be seen in the 'Negative' Bowl, 2005 by Ane Christensen; and scoring to create an indent before folding the silver, as illustrated by 'Tilt' Dish, 2009, by Angela Cork. All are part of the repertoire of traditional hand techniques used by silversmiths today. Finally, the process of soldering (to bind components together) is an equally complicated skill to master. Today's designer silversmiths not only employ these hand techniques, but they have the additional advantages of modern equipment and processes. Machines for spinning and stamping, digital rapid prototyping, laser and tungsten inert gas welding, water jet cutting, as well as the use of computer aided design increase the versatility of such workshops to enable them to produce quality modern design in quantity.

The decorative treatments used for silver include

Artist enameller, Jane Short

Craftsman engraving

Artist chaser, Rod Kelly

enamelling, chasing, engraving, modelling and casting. These skills have been used since ancient times and continue to be used today. Hand engraving is the specialist craft of cutting away the surface of silver, to create inscriptions, armorials, or decorative imagery, using a steel graver with the object resting on a pad. A lyrical example of this technique is the 'Honeysuckle' Vase, 2013, by Angus McFadyen. In the commercial world a high percentage of engraving is now done digitally.

Enamelling uses special glass which is ground to a fine powder suspended in water and applied to silver surfaces, using the processes of champlevé, basse taille, cloissoné, or plique-à-jour. The enamel is then fired at a high temperature in a kiln, to fuse the glass to the silver. The latest enamelled acquisition to the Collection is 'Colour Junction', 2015, by Jane Short.

The skill of chasing is personified in the work of Rod Kelly and Michael Lloyd, renowned artist chasers. As an allied craft, chasing is one of the most important skills in silversmithing, offering great diversity of expression in creating form, pattern and detail. It exploits the malleability of silver by embossing its surface using steel chasing punches and specialist hammers, with the object kept still by being fixed in a bowl filled with pitch. A large scale example of chasing is the Diamond Jubilee Dish, 2015, by Rod Kelly.

Artist silversmith, Rauni Higson, raising silver

THE AESTHETIC OF CONCEPTUALISM

The starting point for artist silversmiths is observation and an exploration of an idea, or concept. Drawings are by definition two dimensional representations of these first impressions. Drawings then provide the point of departure towards the making of the idea into a three-dimensional object. The achievement of working in the silver metal is the transformation. The effect that this transformation has on the material, turning the invisible into visible, is realised by skilled, often intuitive, craftsmanship.

The 21st century poses new questions about the role of silver objects and ornaments. What is a vessel? What is a vase? What is needed to make such things resonate to the viewer as functional objects of beauty, and not mere utilitarian items? Part of this resonance is due to the social and cultural identity detectable in the individual creative expressions in silver.

In this exhibition 18 silversmiths are from different cultural backgrounds. Several are from Far-Eastern cultures. People from these cultures feel a sense of profundity in the universe, a sense of a single spirit that the Chinese call 'qi'. Expressing a potential from the nothingness is to connect with this sense of profoundness, and is a connection that underpins art in all Far-Eastern cultures. It is conveyed as a notion and gives an atmosphere to a work in silver. This notion can be seen in 'Aqua-Poesy VII', 2003, by Hiroshi Suzuki, a vase he calls a poetry of water. It can be seen in the abstract evocations of nature expressed in the swirling forms used in the silver work of the Korean silversmiths William Lee and Kyosun Jung, or in the organic 'marine shape' of the box by the Chinese silversmith, Nan Nan Liu.

In the West, the intuitive response by artist silversmiths to their subject matter has no universal spiritual cultural perimeter. Instead it is the personal exploration of the individual artist silversmith's response to nature's beauty, or his or her response to cerebral notions of negative space, deconstruction of form and the relationships of shape. There is a feeling of trying to write originally in silver to create a visual form of writing in a language of technique. Theirs is a personal expression at a human level. Inspiration comes from observation. The breaking of ocean waves is studied by Miriam Hanid; the structure of a railway viaduct is related in a innovative set of cutlery by Petya Kapralova; and a plant emerging from a rocky Welsh quarry face leads to a silver vase by Rauni Higson. Thus artist craftsman silversmiths observe to distil a concept, which is realised through their extraordinary craft skills.

'Persephone' Vase, 2012 by Rauni Higson

'Aqua-Poesy VII' Vase, 2003 by Hiroshi Suzuki

Drawing by Michael Lloyd from his sketchbook

CONCLUSION

What then is the value of a silver beaker today by the artist silversmith Michael Lloyd? Is it the material of silver? Is it the skilful hand-chasing of the imagery or is it his creative artistry?

To answer these questions more fully, the initial idea of the beaker's design, and the translation of that design into the finished, chased piece are two sides of the same coin. Between them, they provide the creative artistry. For the artist silversmith there is no distinction between art and craft; they are inextricably welded together. The silver metal has a material value, but for the artist silversmith, the silver – that malleable, lustrous, enduring metal – is simply the vehicle for realising the design through the employment of the relevant craft skills. In one sense, the value of a Michael Lloyd beaker is an amalgam of all three elements, but in another sense it is none of these. The real value of the beaker lies in just two words: Michael Lloyd, just in the same way that the signature of David Hockney on one of his paintings defines the value of that painting.

Behind the world of the artisan is that sustainable energy, the motivation – it has been there so long; that desire to take an inanimate material, and bring it to life in a form or image that will sing out; that desire to pay homage to my surroundings, to my creativity; that thanksgiving to that first bite into the apple of awareness ... And what of the work? It is simply my response to cherished observations.

These poetic words of the silversmith Michael Lloyd, so admired by his peers, resonates with all those silversmiths represented in this exhibition. Their work is a beacon, highlighting a new creative movement in silver, a renaissance of this ancient discipline happening in Britain today. Indeed, their discipline from now on should always be known as 'The Silversmith's Art'.

Opposite: Detail from Vase by Angus McFadyen

CATALOGUE

MALCOLM APPLEBY

'Making and creating is part of my daily cycle. Inspiration can come from anywhere; I can turn a political catchphrase such as "The Enemy Within" into a lettering design for one of my silver beakers. The making process is an inspiration in itself. I much prefer natural forms and textures to industrial forms and polished surfaces, frequently distorting the silver using corroded tools. These make subtle textures and informal surfaces over which I can engrave.'

Born 1946. Attended the Royal College of Art, 1968. Awarded an MBE in 2014 for services to Hand Engraving. Tutor and Honorary Fellow of Bishopsland Educational Trust. Lifetime achievement Award from the Hand Engravers Association of Great Britain.

Originally a part time apprentice to John Wilkes, gunsmiths; learning the highly formalized art of engraved gun decoration, Malcolm Appleby is now a renowned artist engraver of silver, gold, platinum, steel, iron and bronze. His work covers gun engraving, jewellery, art medals, silversmithing and printmaking. An exceptional creative draughtsman, his work is made in his studio workshop in Scotland.

Public Collections include:
1978 Gold Feather Necklace, Aberdeen Art Gallery, Aberdeen;
1985 Seal, for the Board of Trustees, the Victoria and Albert Museum, London;
1986 The 'Raven Gun', the Royal Armouries, The Tower of London, London;
1989 Standing Cup and Cover, National Museums Scotland, Edinburgh;
1990 Cake Slice, The Rabinovitch Collection at the Victoria and Albert Museum, London;
2000 Tea Pot and Bowl, Perth Art Gallery and Museum, Perth;
2006 'Swan' Bowl, Ashmolean Museum, Oxford;
2007 Design for 150th Years Celebration Book, the Victoria and Albert Museum, London.

Selected Commissions include:
1969 Orb, HRH The Prince of Wales' Coronet;
1978 King George VI and Queen Elizabeth Diamond Stakes Trophy ,

De Beers, London;
1986 'Fall Out' Medal, British Art Medal Society, London;
1987 Condiment Set, The Silver Trust for No.10 Downing Street, London;
1991 Diamond Jubilee Medal, The National Trust for Scotland;
1999 Sculptural Table Piece, commissioned by the Incorporation of Goldsmiths, Edinburgh and loaned to Bute House, Edinburgh;
2000 Royal Medals, The Royal Society of Edinburgh;
2005 The Trafalgar Medal, Sim Comfort Associates;
2009 'Modern Nautilus' Loving Cups, George Heriot School Trust, Edinburgh;
2012 Medal for XXXII Fidem Art Medal Congress, University of Glasgow;
2013 Pair of Candlesticks, St Giles' Cathedral, Edinburgh.

The Goldsmiths' Company Modern Silver Collection (not included in the exhibition):
1969 Cigar Jar;
1970 Ring Box;
1978 Commemorative Bowl to mark 500 years since the London Assay Office was established at Goldsmiths' Hall;
1988 Two Bowls;
1991 Cigar Box;
1992 Charger.

Malcolm Appleby's numerous private commissions cannot be recorded here, however it should be noted that one such commission, The Prince of Wales' Gold Cup, 1970, engraved with Prince of Wales feathers, lion, unicorn and dragon imagery, and made when he was only 23 years old, was sold at Bonhams' 'Distinguished Designs and Post-War Silver' auction in November 2011 for £78,000, setting a new record for post-war silver or gold.

Detail

'THE MILLENNIUM CASKET', 1999

18 carat white and yellow gold casket designed and engraved by Malcolm Appleby. Seamed and raised, base of Turkish burr walnut with large Indian moonstone set in lid, made by Hector Miller, silversmith.
Millennium Commission
Marks: Malcolm Appleby, Edinburgh
Height 11cm · length 17cm

Engraved with a rising and setting sun above the ocean, which symbolise the passage of time throughout the seasons. The moonstone is evocative of the moon's influence on the tides and enhances the imagery of the fundamental elements required to support life of fire, water, air and light. The casket is for wild flower seeds which were sown in the millennium year as a symbol of regeneration of the precious planet earth in the 21st century.

BEAKER, 2004

Sawn, slashed and soldered, burnished parcel-gilt finish assisted by Peter Musgrove, silversmith.
Purchase
Marks: Malcolm Appleby, Edinburgh
Height 7.5cm · diameter 8.5cm

Part of a series of 'slashed' beakers, which demonstrate Malcolm Appleby's interest in experimenting with unconventional techniques. Here the inspiration came from the splits that can mistakenly occur in beakers when they are being hand-made. Deliberately sawing and slashing the metal, Appleby soldered the beaker back together to create a unique finished surface with subtle engraved decoration at the foot.

TUMBLER CUP, 2010

Raised with creased lip, gilt interior with swirling hammer texture.
Purchase
Marks: Malcolm Appleby, Edinburgh
Height 7cm · diameter 8.5cm

One of hundreds of tumbler cups made by Malcolm Appleby. This cup was made in Appleby's workshop by Callum Strong, apprentice, under Appleby's instruction using a specialist hammer to create the texture. Callum was asked to 'draw with the hammer'. The characteristic of these tumbler cups is the unique finishing of the edges, giving the holder a tactile sense of the complete object in their hand. This Tumbler Cup was purchased through John Higgins' Contemporary Silver Gallery, in 2011.

'TECTONIC' BEAKERS I AND II, 2014

Britannia silver. Part raised by Peter Musgrove, silversmith. Shaped and finished by Malcolm Appleby using ridged-inside stakes and rusty hammers. Enamel with gold leaf by Jane Short, enameller.
Purchase
Marks: Malcolm Appleby, Edinburgh
Height 7.2cm · diameter 8.5cm

Using different metals and collaborating with other craftsmen has been a core interest of Appleby. Here he invited the renowned artist enameller Jane Short to work with him and undertake a technical challenge in enamelling.

He asked Jane to interpret freely the steel and gold fired colours that he creates in his workshop, using gold foils and enamel on silver and using the reflective qualities of part-enamelling the inside surfaces of the vessel. The beakers evoke a vision in enamel of gold melting in fire, and in a wider context, a vision of volcanic activity of tectonic plates shifting in our planet.

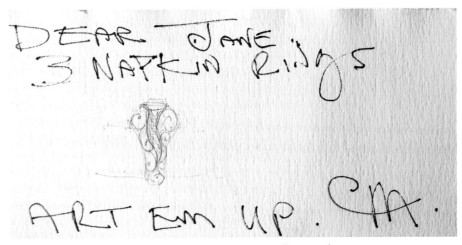

Example of Malcolm Appleby's artistic instruction to enameller Jane Short.

ALEX BROGDEN

'My fascination with both natural geometry and the vessels and architecture of antiquity, combine to inspire my work. By transforming the fluidity of the smoothly controlled carving of wax into the hard permanence of metal, I aim to hold onto the spontaneity of an idea through the long process of realising a work in silver. Strength of form and fineness of finish are what I strive for.'

Born 1954. Master's degree, Royal College of Art, 1986. Consultant Silver Advisor to the Goldsmiths' Company's Modern Collection Committee, 2004–2010.

Alongside traditional silversmithing techniques, Brogden has developed unique methods for controlling the hand carving of wax which, after casting or electroforming, often forms a part of his pieces. His studio workshop is in Sheffield.

Public Collections include:
1993 Large Fluted Bowl, The Crafts Council, London;
1994 Fluted Bowl, Shipley Art Gallery, Gateshead;
1996 Fish Server, The Rabinovitch Collection at the Victoria and Albert Museum, London;
2005 Cutlery and Bowl, Sheffield Museums Trust, Sheffield;
2008 Large Fluted Bowl, Fitzwilliam Museum, Cambridge.

Selected Commissions include:
1990 Three Large Centrepieces, Mr Nicola Bulgari;
1991 Pair of Candelabra, The Silver Trust for No.10 Downing Street, London;
1993 Processional Cross, St Denys' Church, Sleaford;
1997 Candlesticks, The Pearson Collection;
1999 Pair of Processional Tapers, Lichfield Cathedral;
1999 Rosewater Dish, Corpus Christi College, Cambridge;
1999 'The Sweeny Cup', The Royal College of Physicians, London;
2000 Nave Altar Cross and Candlesticks, York Minster;
2003 Chalice, St Albans Cathedral;
2003 Rosewater Dish, The Worshipful Company of Haberdashers, London;
2004 Rosewater Dish, The Worshipful Company of Clothworkers, London;
2009 Covered Cup, The Fox Club, London;
2010 Three Pairs of Candlesticks, The Society of Dilettanti, London;
2011–12 Three Pairs of Candelabra, The Worshipful Company of Haberdashers, London;
2013 Lectern, The Worshipful Company of Coopers, London;
2014 'Continuum' Table Sculpture, Trinity Hall College, Cambridge.

The Goldsmiths' Company Modern Silver Collection (not included in the exhibition):
1990 Dish;
1996 Rosewater Dish;
2011 Replica of the Corieltavi Bowl.

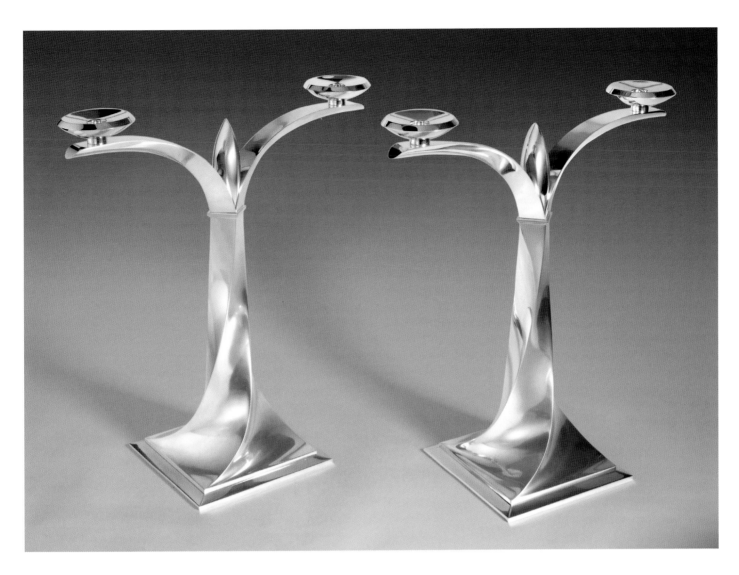

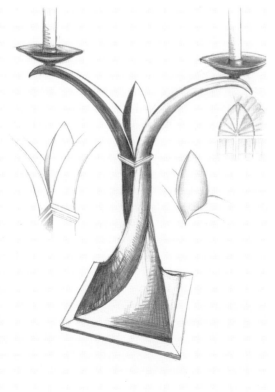

Drawing

PAIR OF TWO-LIGHT CANDELABRA, 2006

Spiral stems carved and electroformed, other sections forged, hammered and spun.
Commission
Marks: Alex Brogden, Sheffield
Height 44.1cm · width 42cm

Commissioned to commemorate the year of office of Mr David Peake as Prime Warden of the Goldsmiths' Company, 2003–2004, for use at Livery Dinners at Goldsmiths' Hall. The central motif of a lotus bud refers to Mr Peake's country estate in Gloucestershire, Sezincote. Built in 1805 by Samuel Pepys Cockerell, Humphrey Repton designed its landscape incorporating Indian Hindu styled elements. In the Hindu religion the sacred lotus bud symbolises potential, specifically in a spiritual nature.

VASE, 2015

*Vase body produced by first hand carving the
form in wax. It is then electroformed with a
thick, rough layer of silver. This silver form
is then refined by a long process of filing and
abrasion; the foot and neck are then fabricated.
Highly polished finish by Elliot Fitzpatrick.
Commission
Marks: Alex Brogden, Sheffield
Height 30cm · diameter 20.4cm*

This piece, in the form of a polyhedron
(gyrate rhombicosidodecahedron);
a 'Johnson Solid' form consisting of
20 regular triangular faces, 30 square
faces, 12 regular pentagonal faces, 60
vertices and 120 edges. The vase is
the latest development in a sequence
of pieces by Alex Brogden, featuring
highly geometric faceted forms. The
series exploits wax carving techniques
which he has developed over the last
three decades. The methods allow the
making of innovative silver forms, the
production of which is unsuited to
other techniques.

The vase was commissioned for a
new display in 2015 of contemporary
designed pieces by modern silversmiths.
This display, known as the Buffet
Plate, will be used at Goldsmiths' Hall
to highlight the Company's role as a
major patron of modern silver and the
exceptional quality of the silver work.

The term buffet plate is explained
as follows. Since the Middle Ages,
buffets, or sideboards, have been used
in grand dining rooms to display and
store utilitarian silver items such as
ewers and basins, flagons and dishes.
These large items were referred to
simply as plate, from the Spanish 'plata',
meaning silver.

CLIVE BURR

'As a small boy, my first experience of metalwork was of welding a go-cart together, with my grandfather. I believe he was my inspiration for becoming a silversmith. Shape, form and function are the key elements in all of my designs. I have a keen interest in all aspects of architecture and find inspiration from these large-scale works of art. I always endeavour to design things in a classic, timeless style, (not necessarily fashion led), and emphatically made to the highest possible standard.'

Born 1953. Master's degree, Royal College of Art, 1979. Chairman of the Contemporary British Silversmiths 2011–2014. Consultant Silver Advisor to the Goldsmiths' Company's Modern Collection Committee 2010 to present day.

Designer silversmith with a design workshop in the City of London employing five skilled craftsmen specialising in small production runs for corporations and other clients as well as domestic silver and one-off commissions.

Public Collections include:
1980 Box, Bristol City Museum and Art Gallery;
2005 'Four Seasons Tazza' (collaboration with Jane Short, enameller), The Keatley Trust at the Victoria and Albert Museum, London;

Selected Commissions include:
1986 Presentation Box, for HM Queen Elizabeth II;
1999 King George VI and Queen Elizabeth Diamond Stakes Trophy , De Beers, London;
2001 Presentation Salver for HM Queen Elizabeth The Queen Mother, De Beers, London;
2002 Mantelpiece Clock, (collaboration with Jane Short, enameller), The Silver Trust for No.10 Downing Street, London;
2006 Box, The Pearson Collection;
2007 Sovereign Box, The Royal Mint, London;
2007–08 Two Ceremonial Maces for Edge Hill University, Lancashire;
2009 Centrepiece (with Jane Short, enameller), The Worshipful Company of Clothworkers;

2010 Bowl presented to James Wolfensohn, Schroders Plc, London;
2010 UAE Presidents Cup series Trophy;
2011 Mace, Perdana University, Kuala Lumpur;
2012 Bell Push (collaboration with Jane Short, enameller), Duke of Devonshire;
2012 Daphne Brooch, Gift for HRH Princesss Alexandra on the opening of The Goldsmiths' Centre;
2013 Clock, The Worshipful Company of Information Technologists;
2014 Clock, The Pearson Collection.

The Goldsmiths' Company Modern Silver Collection (not included in the exhibition):
1984 Clock;
1994 Pepper Mill;
1997 Clock.

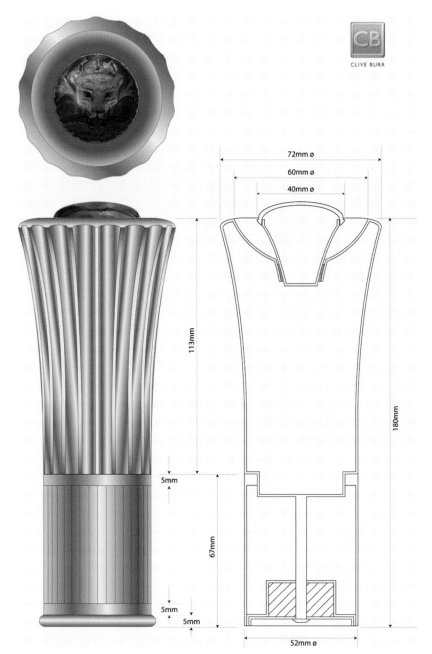

TWO PEPPERMILLS, 2003

*Fabricated, with hand-chased flutes on main
body, engine-turned flutes around base.
Internal ceramic mechanism. Champlevé
enamel leopard head finials by Jane Short,
enameller.*
Commission
Marks: Clive Burr, London
Height 17.5cm · diameter 7.3cm

Two from a set of eight mills
commissioned to commemorate
the year of office of The Rt.Hon. Sir
Adam Butler, as Prime Warden of The
Goldsmiths' Company, 1999–2000, for
use for grinding black pepper at Livery
Dinners at Goldsmiths' Hall.

Design drawing

JOCELYN BURTON

'I wanted to be a painter but the prospects
for a woman in the 1960s were bleak.
Silversmithing at the time was a blank
page and I wrote on it. As the years have
gone by my passion for the craft and its
history has increased. My inspiration
springs from nature, life and experience.
Because my work is sometimes complex, an
intricate design is pivotal. I make detailed
pre-calculations and working drawings
some of which are considered works of art
in themselves.

My favourite pieces are usually the ones
I am working on at the moment.'

Born 1946. Trained at the Sir John Cass
College under Jack Stapley. Winner of
the Prince Philip City and Guilds Gold
Medal, 2004. In both 1967 and 1997
winner of the De Beers International
Award for the design of diamond
Jewellery.

Jocelyn Burton founded her studio
workshop in London in 1970 and
established a reputation for large
decorative silver for city institutions
and the Church. Today she specialises
in impressive light fittings for private
clients in grand country houses both in
the United Kingdom and abroad.

Public Collections include:
1983 Architectural Centrepiece,
commissioned by Sir Roy Strong (then
Director), the Victoria and Albert
Museum, London;
1998 The Jerwood Necklace, The
Fitzwilliam Museum, Cambridge;
2011 Pair of 'Surtout de Table' and
a pair of silver gilt fruit bowl covers,
The Farringdon Collection;

Selected Commissions include:
1973 Set of Goblets, St Paul's Cathedral,
London;
1973 Set of Medals, (collaboration with
Henry Moore), Chichester Cathedral;
1979 Salt, Pepper and Mustard on Stand,
The Worshipful Company of Butchers,
London;
1980 King George VI and Queen
Elizabeth Stakes Trophy for De Beers,
Ascot;
1986 Loving Cup with Seahorse Stem,
HM The Queen;
1991 Pair of Candelabra, the Silver Trust
for No.10 Downing Street, London;
1995 Large Dolphin Wall Sconces,
The Worshipful Company of
Fishmongers, London;

Drawing

1995 Offertory Salver, Lichfield
Cathedral;
2000 Processional Torcheres,
York Minster;
2000 Bowl, The Worshipful Company
of Haberdashers to celebrate the
Millennium;
2000 Bowl, The Worshipful Company
of Painter-Stainers to celebrate the
Millennium;
2002 Box, designed for the Millenium,
The Pearson Collection;
2014 'Surtout de Table', The Chelsea
Arts Club, London.

*The Goldsmiths' Company Modern Silver
Collection (not included in the exhibition):*
1975 Cup and cover;
1983 Dish;
1985 Commemorative Bowl;
1988 Wall Sconces.

PAIR OF CANDELABRA, 2003

Fabricated from sheet, scored, folded and soldered. The candle nozzles modelled and cast with spun candle holders. The urn finials fabricated from sheet.
Commission

Marks: NVB for Jocelyn Burton, London Height 54.2cm · width 42.5cm

Commissioned to commemorate the year of office of Mr Richard Vanderpump as Prime Warden of The Goldsmiths' Company, 1998–1999, for use at Livery Dinners at Goldsmiths' Hall. Mr Vanderpump's love of antique silver, particularly The Goldsmiths' Company's six table candelabra of 1740 by Humphrey Payne, was the background brief to this commission.

JULIE CHAMBERLAIN

'Ideas of vessel and function, both notional and specific, are a constant within my work. These ideas are explored with concern for compositional balance, proportion and line and an interest in the relationship objects have to the surface they sit on and the space around them... Full size "sketch" models, whether a fold of paper or a carefully constructed model, are generally how I explore and "play" with the possibilities of an idea or problem once the concept is established.'

Born 1958. Graduate of Middlesex University, 1980. Master's degree, Royal College of Art,1984. Chairman of Contemporary British Silversmiths 2005–2008. Senior Lecturer, BA (Hons) Interior Design and Interior Architecture at Middlesex University 2010 – present day.

An artist silversmith whose interest when designing silver is to rely upon form rather than decoration for visual impact. Julie Chamberlain's studio workshop is in London

Selected Commissions include:
1995 King George VI and Queen Elizabeth Diamond Stakes Trophy, De Beers;
1997 Spoon, The Millennium Canteen for Sheffield City Council;
2000 '2000 AD Commemorative Dish', Lancashire County Council;
2000 Drinking Set, Yorkshire Artspace.

The Goldsmiths' Company Modern Silver Collection (not included in the exhibition):
1994 'Bon Bon' Dish.

'OBLIQUE' DISH, 2006

Fabricated from silver sheet, soldered in sections.
Commission
Marks: Julie Chamberlain, London
Height 7cm · width 16cm

Commissioned following the exhibition 'Contemporary London Silversmiths' at Norman Adams, Fine Art and Antique Dealer, in 2006.

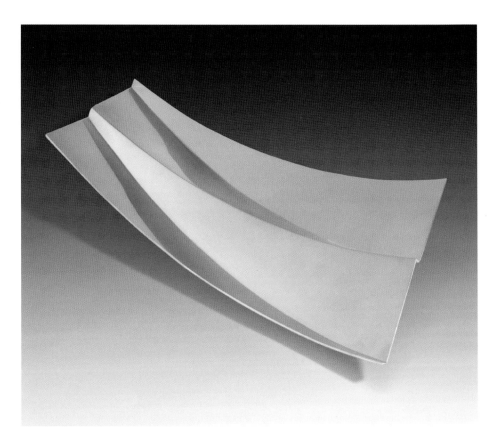

ANE CHRISTENSEN

'My work explores the boundaries between functionality and sculptural form.

The starting point for all my work is the simple geometry of spun forms, tubing and flat sheet, which I then "interrupt" and deconstruct using piercing, scoring and folding and hand forming.

I continue to draw inspiration for my work from the urban landscape. Especially from building sites, "negative spaces" between buildings and architectural decay.

Born Denmark, 1972. Master's degree, Royal College of Art, 1999. Bishopsland Educational Trust Senior Fellow.

An artist silversmith whose interests focus on the principle of restriction and the extension of the possibilities within such a constraint when designing and working with silver. Ane Christensen's starting point is working with a single sheet of metal as her work extends also to non-precious metals. Resident in England, Ane's studio workshop is in London.

Public Collections include:
2002 'Floating Bowl', The P&O Makower Trust donated to The Crafts Council, London;
2003 Fish Server, The Rabinovitch Collection at the Victoria and Albert Museum, London;
2003 'Symbiosis No.1' Bowl, Birmingham Museum and Art Gallery, Birmingham;
2005 Patinated Copper Negative Bowl and 'One Meter Fish Slice' Museum of Decorative Arts, Copenhagen, Denmark;
2005 'Dented' Bowl, The Pearson Collection;
2005 Pair of 'Dented' Bowls, Fitzwilliam Museum, Cambridge;
2006 Large Sterling Silver 'Dented' Bowl, Koldinghus Museum, Kolding, Denmark.

'DENTED' BOWL, 2003

Spun and pierced using a single sheet of silver. Commission
Marks: Ane Christensen, London
Height 13cm · diameter 25.6cm

Emphasising, equally, function and sculpture, the starting point is a 'perfect' bowl, which then is partly deconstructed. The piece explores the tension between contrasting elements within a simple form.

Purchased through 'The Metal Gallery', Mount Street, London.

'NEGATIVE' BOWL, 2005

*Spun and hand-pierced from a single sheet
of silver.*
Purchase
Marks: Ane Christensen, London.
Height 11cm · diameter 25.2cm

Ane Christensen's examination of
the bowl form starts with a strictly
economical use of material, dealing
with transformation and restricted
space to produce a highly structured
work, retaining qualities of tension and
strength within the form to give it a
new direction.

'CRUMBLING' BOWL, 2006

Spun, fabricated and drilled.
Purchase
Marks: Ane Christensen, London
Height 10cm · diameter 23cm

Ane Christensen was short-listed for
the Jerwood Applied Arts Prize 2005.
This bowl was purchased following
the exhibition of her new work for this
prestigious prize. It demonstrates one of
her innovative explorations of the bowl
form, deliberately made from one sheet
of silver as an exercise in restriction
and creativity.

DAVID CLARKE

'The conservativeness of the discipline (of silver) really pushes me to become more creative, challenging and playful. It is essential to keep this discipline alive and forward thinking.'

Born 1967. Master's degree, Royal College of Art, 1997. Senior Fellow of Bishopsland Educational Trust. The final function of an object, its use and setting and the process of bringing something new to the standard expectation of an object is always the starting point for this silversmith. David Clarke's studio workshop is in London.

Public Collections include:
1998 Fruit stand, the Victoria and Albert Museum, London;
2000 Three Vases, The Crafts Council, London;
2002 Fish Slice, The Rabinovitch Collection at the Victoria and Albert Museum, London;
2003 Three Candle Holders 2003, Shipley Art Gallery, Gateshead;
2004 '173' Platter, the Victoria and Albert Museum, London;
2002 'Field of Silver' Project, Birmingham Museum and Art Gallery;
2005 'Cut and Shut' Platter, Birmingham Museum and Art Gallery;
2006 'Slightly Sloshed' Beakers, The Marzee Collection, The Netherlands;
2007 'Yea Ha!' Teapot, The Marzee Collection, The Netherlands;
2007 'Brouhaha' Teapot, the Victoria and Albert Museum, London;
2007 'Hang on I'm Coming' Jug, Swaledale Lead Museum, Yorkshire;
2012 'Spoonie' Spoons, The Crafts Council, London;
2012 'Dead On Arrival' Boxed Tea Set, Röhsska Museum, Göteborg;
2013 'Brouhaha' Teapot, The National Museum, Oslo;
2014 'I Want More!' Spoons, The National Museum Northern Ireland;
2014 'Feed Me!' Spoons, Brighton Museum and Art Gallery;

2014 'Hang on I'm Coming' Jug, Hiko Mizuno Collection, Tokyo.

Selected Commissions include:
2000 Two Rose Bowls to celebrate the University of Central Lancashire's award for 'The Freedom of the City';
2002 Fruit Centrepiece, The British Council, London.

The Goldsmiths' Company Modern Silver Collection (not included in the exhibition):
1999 Fruit Stand

'CUT AND SHUT' PLATTER, 2006

Hand sawn wires directly cut from line drawing on sheet silver. Each cut element is filed, laid exposing the sawn edge, and then soldered together in the order of the original cut elements. The platter is then heated and immersed in dilute sulphuric acid bringing the fine silver content to the surface to give a white finish, then taken back to a final matt and silver finish.
Commission
Marks: David Clarke, London
Height 6cm · length 53.1cm · width 19cm

This new series of platters came from David Clarke going back to basics and looking at the potential for piercing a sheet of silver. Within this work there is the notion of freedom and spontaneity, gesturing to the rawness of a landscape. Displays of fruit and nuts have to be carefully arranged with the platter dictating their position.

KEVIN COATES

'Part of the joy of history is finding the links of similarities and finding the links of us and those who have gone before... as an artist I am released from the responsibilities that I would have otherwise had if I were presenting scholarship... my aim has always been to stimulate a new journey of connection both for the viewer and of course myself.'

Born 1950. Master's degree, Royal College of Art, 1976. PhD, Royal College of Art, 1979. Associate Artist at The Wallace Collection, London 2007–2011, which culminated in his one-man show, 'Time Regained'.

Working from his studio workshop in London, Kevin Coates is an artist craftsman whose intellectual and creative treatment of subject matter combined with a technical excellence of modelling places him outside any style time-frame, whether making large pieces or jewellery.

Public Collections include:
1982 'Athene Noctua' Brooch, the Victoria and Albert Museum, London;
1982 'Seraph' Brooch, the Victoria and Albert Museum, London;
1982 'Caliban' Ring, the Victoria and Albert Museum, London;
1986 'The Carrington Cup', the Victoria and Albert Museum, London;
1987 'Monahan Medal', The British Museum, London;
1991 'Mozart Medal', The British Museum, London;
1992 Cake Slice, The Rabinovitch Collection at the Victoria and Albert Museum, London;
1994 Centrepiece, Leeds Castle;
1998 'Frog Labyrinth' Brooch, Spencer Museum of Art, University of Kansas, Lawrence;
1999 'Entry of the Queen of the Night' Tiara, National Museums Scotland, Edinburgh;
2002 'Waiting for Joan' Brooch, National Museums Scotland, Edinburgh;
2006 'Pan' Ring, from 'An Alphabet of Rings', Daphne Farago Collection, Museum of Fine Arts, Boston;

2010 'Eye of God' Ring, Ashmolean Museum, Oxford;
2011 'The Weighing of the Heart' Wall-Mounted Brooch, The Smithsonian Institution, Cooper Hewitt Museum, New York;
2014 'A (Second) Rabbit for Fibonacci' from 'A Bestiary of Jewels', Ashmolean Museum, Oxford.

Public Commissions include:
1982 King George VI and Queen Elizabeth Diamond Stakes Trophy 1982, De Beers, London;
1983 The British Society for the History of Pharmacy, London – Presidential Badge;
1984 'The Maze Centre-piece' (Memorial to Peter Wilson), Leeds Castle;
1990 'The St Chad's Cup', Lichfield Cathedral;
1991 St. George Centre-piece, The Silver Trust for No.10 Downing Street;
2002 'The Flood Centrepiece', Schroders Bank.

The Goldsmiths' Company Modern Silver Collection (not included in the exhibition):
1982 Cup;
1982 De Beers Ascot Trophy;
1988 Rosewater Dish.

'THE CHARTER BELL', 2003

Double bell, 18 carat gold, silver gilt, lapis lazuli, blackstone, stainless steel double bell.
Commission
Marks: Kevin Coates, London & signed "Coates 02".
Height 39cm · diameter 23cm

The 12 zodiac houses are depicted in silver gilt on a background of lapis lazuli and are arranged as they were at the time of the Goldsmiths'Company's first Royal Charter of 15th March, 1327. The Charter gave legal existence to this ancient guild, which still today continues to carry out its traditions of hallmarking and support of the goldsmithing craft.

The base is inscribed 'By touch of stone I sound for man the truth of noble metal: such gold and silver are, in turn, the test of man's own mettle', and below the demi-virgin finial, the Goldsmiths' Company's crest, 'First Royal Charter 15th March 1327'. The main body is decorated with the astrological chart for that date. The bell is rung at the Court of Assistants meeting when a new Prime Warden is elected each year in May, the concept of time present and time past is thus marked.

ROSAMOND CONWAY

Enamel test pieces

'*Enamelling is one of those crafts that you never fully learn, you think you have it mastered but you don't. You need a lot of patience*'.

Born 1951. Master's degree, Royal College of Art, 1975. Senior lecturer at Middlesex University, 1986–2011.

Rosamond Conway's studio workshop is situated close to her Rhine barge moored in the tidal estuary of the River Deben in Suffolk which she overlooks from her window. Her profound sensitivity to her surroundings of nature is translated first into delicate drawings and watercolours and then into silver with use of enamel processes.

Public Collections include:
1978 Two Brooches, Birmingham Museum and Art Gallery, Birmingham;
1979 Brooch, Birmingham Museum and Art Gallery, Birmingham;
1980 'Inlaid' Necklace, Leeds City Art Gallery, Leeds;
1984 Enamelled Brooch, the Victoria and Albert Museum, London;
1994 Fish Slice, The Rabinovitch Collection at the Victoria and Albert Museum, London;
2009 'Pate de Verre' Vessel (made 1997), Dan Klein and Alan J Poole Collection, National Museums Scotland, Edinburgh;
2014 Enamel Brooch, Ros Conway and Hugh Donnell, 1984, The Los Angeles County Museum of Fine Art, USA;
2014 Enamel Brooch, Ros Conway and Hugh Donnell, 1984, The Museum of Fine Arts, Houston, Texas.

Detail sketchbook drawing

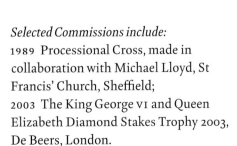

Selected Commissions include:
1989 Processional Cross, made in collaboration with Michael Lloyd, St Francis' Church, Sheffield;
2003 The King George VI and Queen Elizabeth Diamond Stakes Trophy 2003, De Beers, London.

The Goldsmiths' Company Modern Silver Collection (not included in the exhibition):
1993 Two Salts and Spoons.

Drawings from sketchbook

WAFER BOX, 2008

Enamelled box with boxwood interior to contain the wafers in tooled slots. The image is a summary of pencil and watercolour drawings. Silversmithing by Clive Burr, the symbolic triangular form first tooled in steel with the aid of CAD technology in order to have a box and lid of an exact fit, the silver is then stamped to provide a smooth silver surface for the basse-taille and cloisonné enamel work by Rosamond Conway.
Commission
Marks: Rosamond Conway, London
Height 4.3cm · width 15.5cm

Rosamond Conway, inspired by the River Deben in Suffolk where she lives and works, uses wild river bank plants such as wild carrot and dandelion in a circular design in autumnal colours evoking the passage of time with a central motif of three fish swimming in a circle for the Resurrection.

Wafer boxes are used to store wafers (usually made from wheat flour and water) which are eaten during the service of Holy Communion. During Holy Communion in the Church of England, the 'communicant' receives a wafer to symbolise Jesus' body.

The church since the late 20th century has embraced commissioning contemporary silver for new ecclesiastical silver as the artist silversmiths express the faith today in their designs. Often these new commissions result as a consequence of a visit to see the Goldsmiths' Company's Collection by the dean of a cathedral or a vicar of a local parish church.

ANGELA CORK

'While much of the inspiration for my work derives from studying architectural forms and structured spaces like Japanese gardens, I find inspiration in almost anything. Prior to my training to be a silversmith I took design courses with a graphics based content, and this was when I really developed my personal visual language. I often dissect what I am looking at, picking out details that I like. I repeatedly see sculptural contrast and arrangements within a shape and surface, and I have a fascination with representing this into interesting new compositions and concepts.'

Born 1973. Master's degree, Royal College of Art, 2002. Bishopsland Educational Trust, 1998–2000. Current Senior Fellow and Tutor, Bishopsland Educational Trust. Part time tutor, London Arts Com, Central St Martins, London, 2004 – present day. Artist silversmith in residence for the Goldsmiths' Company's exhibition, 'Studio Silver Today', at Belton House, Lincolnshire, in liaison with the National Trust, 2014.

An artist silversmith who specialises in contemporary sculptural vessels largely constructed by hand fabrication. Angela Cork's studio workshop is in London.

Public Collections include:
1998 Brass, Copper and White Metal Tray, The Friends of Glasgow School of Art;
2000 Raised Rocking Bowl, Birmingham Museum and City Art Gallery;
2000 Five-Piece Cutlery Set, Birmingham Museum and City Art Gallery;
2007 'Shift' Vase, P&O Makower Trust, donated to the National Museum Wales, Cardiff.

Selected Commissions include:
1997 The Sir Herbert Read Award, International Society for Education Through Art;
1999 15 Pharmaceutical Awards, The Financial Times;
2008 'Sir Joseph Larmor's Plate', St John's College, Cambridge;
2009 Vase, The John Downham Award for Excellence, Esomar, Amsterdam;
2009 Vases for The Vineyard Restaurant at Stockcross, Newbury;
2014 Beaker, New College, Oxford.

TWO 'SLIM BALLOON' VASES, 2006

*Central shape flat-hammered over steel
formers to template shape, soldered sides with
burnished edges.*
Commission
Marks: Angela Cork, London
Large vase: Height 25.8cm · width 26.5cm
Small vase: height 20.2cm · width 20.2cm

Angela Cork continues here to develop
the theme of vessel balance for aesthetic
effect. Water and flowers affect the
movement of these heavy vases causing
them to tip dramatically forward.

'FRAME' VASE, 2007

*Frame, silver gilt, fabricated from a heavy gauge
sheet using a box making technique.*
*Water container, silver and oxidised, made
using the method of pressing.*
Commission
Marks: Angela Cork, London
Height 18.5cm · width 2.8cm · length 17.5cm

The conception of what a 'frame' does
inspired this piece where a picture
frame is created to emphasise the flower
making it special.

TWO 'BLOWN' VASES, 2010

Constructed by hammering over formers and by the method of pressing. The interiors of the vessels are oxidised.
Purchase
Marks: Angela Cork, London
Small vase: height 9.5cm · width 6.8cm
Large vase: height 12.7cm · width 9cm

The simplicity and clean lines of the rectangular vases contrast with the organic form of any flowers contained. The side profiles of these vases have a subtle curve that accentuates their volume and produces a sense of fullness as if they have been filled with air, hence their title 'Blown'.

These 'Blown' Vases were purchased from Goldsmiths' Fair, 2010.

'TILT' DISH, 2009

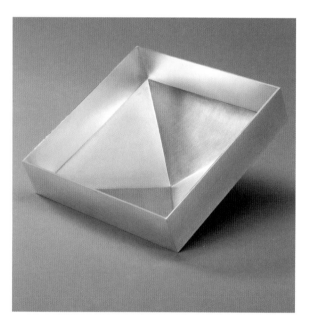

Scored and folded. A small triangle of the base cut and filed away for the addition of the base. The sheet inside the box inserted and recessed into the bottom and stitched in place to ensure its location and soldered from the back.
Purchase
Marks: Angela Cork, London
Height 10.3cm · width 10.7cm

This piece is designed as a container for small sweets and fruits, to offer its contents and present them. The tilting angle of the dish invites the viewer to inspect the contents. When empty it offers an interesting view of what is essentially a simple box balancing on an angle. The pivoting point of the dish provides contact for the tilting angle, but is minimal, to suggest the possibility of a floating box. The base becomes an echo of the form and suggests the shadow of the box.

'Tilt' Dish was purchased at 'Origin', 2011.

'QUADRANGLE' DISH, 2011

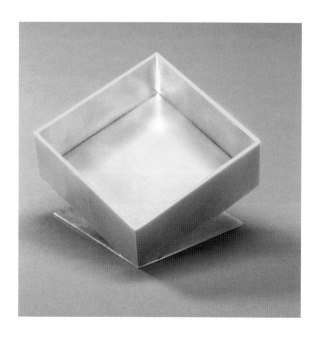

The pyramid centre of the dish is scored and folded, in one piece with a scoring tool of a precise angle. The outer frame is scored and folded separately and the two pieces hand-filed to fit each other exactly.

The final finish is applied with fine industrial scotchbrite pads and coarse grade pumice with soap, and the highly polished edge finished with a steel burnisher by hand.
Purchase
Marks: Angela Cork, London
Height 11.3cm · width 18.4cm

This piece is designed as an occasional dish to offer contents and present them. A variety of silversmithing skills are employed by Angela Cork to create what would appear to the viewer a deceptively simple object.

'Quadrangle' Dish was purchased at 'Origin', 2011.

'FACET' VASE, 2012

Scored and folded. Tapered hexagonal form with two angled bases.
Purchase
Marks: Angela Cork, London
Height 23cm · width 12.5cm

The architectural lines and planes of this form are carefully manipulated to enhance the polished surfaces of this multi-faceted vase, creating a subtle illusion of ambiguity.

The piece is intentionally weighted to lean on a small section of the base to dramatically tilt forward resulting in a sense of movement, and can sit on either side of the base to produce a different angle.

'PILLOW' DISH, 2014

Hammered over formers and press formed.
Purchase
Marks: Angela Cork, London
Height 3.7cm · width 19.0cm

Suggestive of the form of a pillow that has been rested upon. The weight of the contact has displaced the material, pressing it down and producing voluminous sides to the square form.

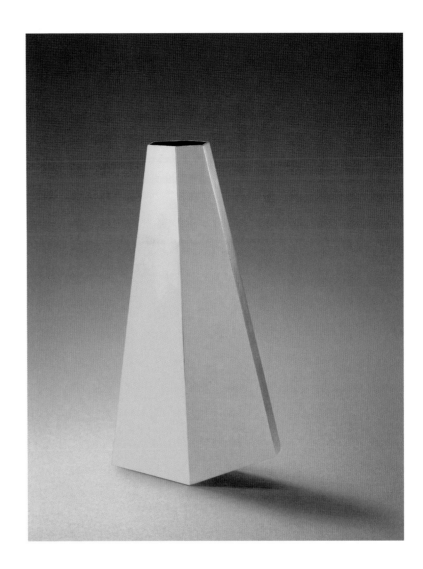

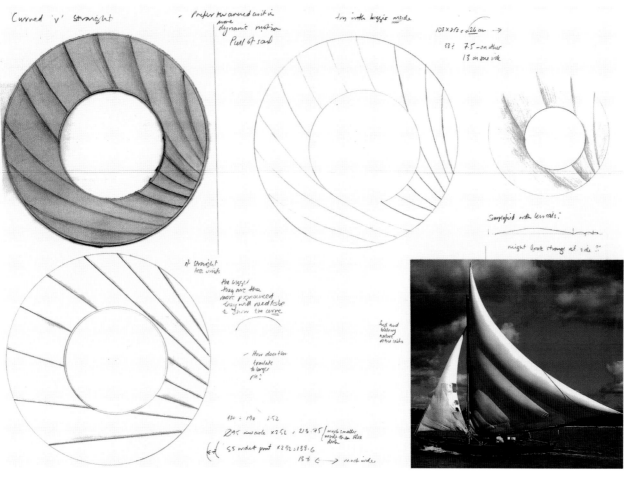

Curved 'V' straight

- Prefer the curved width is more dynamic motion
Pull of sail

try with bigger inside

108 × 212 × 26 cm →

83 ÷ 7.5 = on other
13 on one side

if straight less width

the bigger they are the more pronounced they will need to be & show the curve

- How does this translate to larger pic?

180 ÷ 190   252

295 mire circle × 252 = 213.75 / much smaller inside than disk

55 widest point × 252 = 188.6

13 % ← → much wider

Simplified with less sails:

might look strange at side?

hull and folding nature of the sails

Prime Wardens Sailing boat   - Sail Shapes.

Elegant lines

Almost like Napoleon

Stretch + pull of material

Structure of fabric

Full taught with air volume

Arcs
Swooping curves

interesting lines getting arcs form

sections in the sails are interesting

Sails are almost boat shaped

Shapes in between the sails are interesting too

Drawings and images from sketchbook

ROSEWATER DISH, 2015

Press-formed, spun, soldered and hand-fabricated. Created from 20 separate parts, majority TIG welded together to secure for soldering and traces of the welds later removed. The dish was entirely hand-finished.
Commission
Marks: Angela Cork, London
Height 4.3cm · diameter 48.5cm

Commissioned to commemorate the year of office of Mr Richard Agutter, Prime Warden 2013–2014, for the new buffet plate display. The abstract imagery of the dish is inspired by the formations of sails. This theme was chosen by Mr Agutter as sailing is one of his passions.

REBECCA DE QUIN

'The appearance and working properties of silver make it totally unique and for me it offers enough potential in terms of creative possibilities to last a lifetime. I have always been captivated by the purity and simplicity of silver sheet.

I have found inspiration in formal approaches to painting stemming from the cubist movement, particularly the still-life paintings of the Purists, Ozenfant and Le Corbusier and those of the modernist painter Ben Nicholson whose compositions equally show the influence of cubism. My interest in their two dimensional representations of three dimensional forms leads me to explore object groupings and assemblages that demand attention, by inducing an animated multi-viewpoint experience of changing compositions designed to challenge perceptions of three-dimensional form.'

Born 1958. BA in Three Dimensional Design, Middlesex Polytechnic, 1988. Master's degree, Royal College of Art, 1990. Tutor – Jewellery and Metalwork MA, Royal College of Art, 1998 – present day.

An artist silversmith motivated by the material itself, exploring new and imaginative forms through manipulation of sheet metal by using techniques including cutting, scoring and folding. De Quin works mainly in domestic silverware. Recent pieces indicate new concern with decoration and display through the use of silver combined with other metals, showing some influence from her Belgian father, the constructivist sculptor, Robert de Quin. Her studio workshop is in London.

Public Collections include:
1991 Brown reclining Pomander, Ulster Museum, National Museums Northern Ireland;
1993 Blue reclining Pomander, Shipley Art Gallery, Gateshead;
1998 Jug and Two Beakers with Tray, Silver and Glass, Crafts Council, London;
1999 'Hamburg' Pair of Jugs, National Museums Liverpool;
1999 'Spiral' Fruit/Bread Basket, Brighton Museum and Art Gallery;
2000 Sugar and Cream Set with Tongs, Cheltenham Art Gallery and Museum;
2003 'Spottiswoode' Seven Piece Cutlery Place Setting with Servers, Birmingham Museum and Art Gallery;
2004 Two Jugs, Birmingham Museum and Art Gallery;
2005 Water Jug, Shipley Art Gallery, Gateshead;

2006 Leaning Jug, City of Aberdeen Art Gallery;
2015 'Tall & Small' Jug and Beaker Set, the Victoria and Albert Museum, London.

Selected Commissions include:
2004 Pair of scored and folded Dishes, St Cross College, Oxford;
2006 Millennium Cup, Sheffield Assay Office.

The Goldsmiths' Company Modern Silver Collection (not included in the exhibition):
1994 Bowl.

CENTREPIECE, 2002

Fabricated from two sheets of silver on oblong base. Bottom sheet is satin finished, upper sheet is scored and curved to give slatted appearance and is bright finished. Inscription on two sides of base. 'LORD CUNLIFFE PRIME WARDEN 1997–1998'. 'The nectarine and curious peach into my hands themselves do reach'.
Commission
Marks: Rebecca de Quin, London
Height 15.5cm · length 78cm · width 28cm

Commissioned to commemorate the year of office of Lord Cunliffe, Prime Warden 1997–1998, as a centrepiece and fruit dish. The silver curves, defined edges and reflective surfaces make an original form suggestive of a surreal landscape but evocative of the distinctive green roof of the Commonwealth Institute building of 1962, Kensington High Street, London. Lord Cunliffe, architect, was part of the design team for this iconic building.

TWO WATER JUGS, 2004

Fabricated and seamed with gilded interiors.
Commission
Marks: Rebecca de Quin, London
Height 30cm · width 19.8cm

These jugs represent an exploration of the relationship of geometric form within a vessel.

'BLACKWELL SERIES' TWO VASES, 2008

Bright finished fabricated silver vases with oxidised interior. Industrial press tool used to score and fold patinated copper panels.
Commission
Marks: Rebecca de Quin, London
Vase A (left): Silver vase
Height 15.2cm · length 7cm · width 5cm
Copper surround:
Height 29.3cm · length 16cm · width 6cm
Vase B (right): Silver vase
Height 15.2cm · length 8.5cm · width 5.6cm
Copper surround:
Height 15.7cm · length 12cm · width 27cm

Commissioned following Rebecca de Quin's successful exhibition of new work for the '*Seven Smiths*' exhibition at Blackwell, Cumbria in 2007. The vases evoke nature's regain of an industrial landscape.

THREE 'NESTING' VESSELS, 2011

Seamed construction, matt finish.
Purchase
Marks: Rebecca de Quin, London
Large: height 11cm · width 11.6cm
Medium: height 10cm · width 8.4cm
Small: height 9cm · width 5.6cm

Three 'nesting' vessels of tapering teardrop cross section. De Quin's pleasure in the purity of silver sheet is evident here where she converts something perfectly flat in to three perfect three-dimensional forms that as vessels will hold water or pour cream.

Commissioned following a similar set being included in the Goldsmiths' Company's 'Mindful' exhibition, 2011.

STUART DEVLIN

'I hope that my work reflects four maxims:
That future is much more important than
the past
That creativity is paramount
That skill is fundamental
And that the justification for being a
goldsmith is to enrich the way people live
and work'

Born Australia, 1931. Graduate of the Royal College of Art, 1960. Awarded Harkness Fellowship, Columbia University, New York 1960.

In 1965 Stuart Devlin established a workshop and showroom in Clerkenwell, London, employing 40 craftsmen. He subsequently opened a major shop in Conduit Street, in London's West End. In 1980 he was awarded a CMG for 'Services to Design' and in 1982 granted a Royal Warrant of Appointment, Goldsmith and Jeweller to HM The Queen. In 1988 he was made an Officer of the Order of Australia. He was Prime Warden of the Goldsmiths' Company 1996–1997. In addition to being a silversmith and jeweller, Devlin has designed coins for over 36 countries.

Selected Commissions include:
1972 The Silver Wedding Present from HRH The Prince of Wales to HM The Queen and HRH The Duke of Edinburgh;
1975 The Directors' Dining Room Service, Williams & Glyn's Bank, London;
1981 Table Set, Earl and Countess of Mansfield;
1990 Offertory Salver, Lichfield Cathedral;
1990 Millennium Dish, the Worshipful Company of Information Technologists, London;
1996 Mace, Bath University;
2010 Holy Communion Altar Wine Flagon, Westminster Abbey;
2010 Set of One Pound UK coins representing London, Belfast, Edinburgh and Cardiff, The Royal Mint, London.

The Goldsmiths' Company Modern Silver Collection (not included in the exhibition):
1959 4 Piece Coffee Set;
1965 24 Light Candelabrum;
1965 Cigarette Box;
1965 Bell;
1967 Caddy Spoon;
1969–71 Paper Knife Set;
1973 Salver;
1975 Pair of Candlesticks;
1975–6 Easter Egg Set;
1976 Salver;
1976 Plate;
1983 Rosewater Dish;
1984 Salver.

'MILLENNIUM DISH', 1999

Parcel-gilt dish by Stuart Devlin. Rim and coat of arms carved by Stuart Devlin, electroformed by BJS Company Ltd., spun by Peter Lunn. Engraved inscription by Ray Wilkins of R.H. Wilkins Engravers Ltd.
Inscription: 'IN CELEBRATION OF THE MILLENNIUM, THE CITY OF LONDON AND THE ANCIENT CRAFT OF GOLDSMITHING'.
Millennium Commission
Marks: Stuart Devlin, London
Height 7cm · diameter 77cm

This dish, using a combination of modern technology and traditional silversmithing, is considered by Stuart Devlin to be the most important silver commission he has ever had. The dish is a celebration of the City of London, the home of the Goldsmiths' Company since its Royal Charter in 1327. The architectural rim is composed of 85 buildings existing in the year 2000, symbolising the diversity, history and culture of the City in the last year of the 20th century, bordering on the undulating River Thames.

The centre of the dish incorporates Stuart Devlin's version of the Company's coat of arms with particular attention to the mantling. The coat of arms, with its quartered shield of leopards' heads denoting hallmarking, and cups and buckles denoting patronage of large and small workers in precious metals, emphasises the continuity of the standards of excellence maintained for its craft by this City livery company.

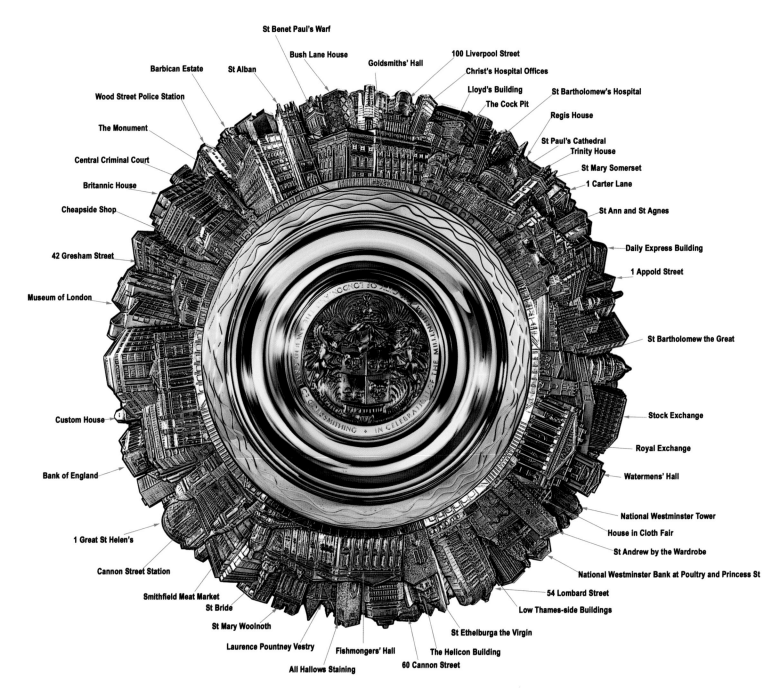

LEXI DICK

'*I aim to make silver that might be dug up with delight long after our civilisation is forgotten. Pieces that do not have to be explained, or put in context. Treasure*'...

Born 1951. Master's degree, Royal College of Art, 1975.

When making silver pieces Lexi Dick focuses on her main discipline of wax modelling, particularly of animals. Her studio workshop is in London.

Public Collections include:
1980 Chain Mail Necklace, The Science Museum, London.

Selected Commissions include:
1987 Pair of Camel Salts, the Worshipful Company of Grocers, London;
1988 Seahorse Bowl, Gift of the Royal Society to Emperor Hirohito of Japan;
1989 Bowl, Gift of the 1922 Committee to Mrs Margaret Thatcher to mark her then ten years in office as Prime Minister;
1991 Offertory Salver, Lichfield Cathedral;
1993 Pair of Fruit Stands, The Silver

Trust for No.10 Downing Street, London;
2002 Winged Horses Centrepiece, Gift of Royal Household to HM The Queen to mark her Majesty's Golden Jubilee;
2002 Ceremonial Salt, the Athenaeum Club, London;
2004 Thirty Candlesticks, the Athenaeum Club, London;
2004 Forty Magnifying Glasses, the Worshipful Company of Grocers, London;
2009 'Griffin' Goblet, the Worshipful Company of Clothmakers, London;
2009 Two Hundred Pendants, the BBC children's programme, 'Keep Your Enemies Close';
2011 Sixteen Camel Salts and Clove

Spoons, the Worshipful Company of Grocers, London;
2014 Two Reticulated Pectoral Crosses, The Bishop of Lincoln;
2014 Five Thousand Gilt Pilgrim Badges, The Historic Lincoln Trust.

The Goldsmiths' Company Modern Silver Collection (not included in the exhibition):
1983 Coaster;
1983 Wine Funnel;
1983 Claret Wine Label;
1983 Wine Taster;
1989 Leopard Bowl;
1990 Unicorn Bowl and Cover;
1994 'Bon Bon' Dish;
1994 Salt and Spoon.

Detail

STANDING SALT, 2005

Spun sections, glass, enamel, amethysts,
diamonds, garnets and citrines, with modelled
and cast animals. Gilded.
Commission
Marks: Lexi Dick, London
Height 35cm · diameter 23cm

Commissioned to commemorate the
year of office of Mr Bruno Schroder
as Prime Warden of the Goldsmiths'
Company, 2001–2002. The design is
inspired by the antique silver pieces in
The Schroder Collection, a collection
of outstanding German Renaissance
goldsmith's work originally formed
by Baron Sir John Henry Schroder
(1825–1910), the London banker. The
unicorns and leopard are taken from
the Goldsmiths' Company's coat of
arms, the dragons represent the City of
London. In England the relative value
of salt and the necessity for its use from
the Middle Ages to flavour food gave
this commodity a place of honour at
the table. The container used to hold
it, the standing salt, thus gained social
importance as well as providing a
practical function. Placed by the host,
the guests were either 'above or below
the salt'.

SIDSEL DORPH-JENSEN

'Silverware is often used in conjunction with celebrating the beautiful and important moments in our lives and I love being the one who creates such objects.

I create objects that show the malleability and organic nature of silver. It is important that the material is relevant to the function of the object, but also that the object can communicate the function. As a designer-silversmith I believe that silver is a very effective medium to express contemporary values.'

THREE VESSELS, 2003

Britannia silver. Raised, hammered and matt finished surface. Solder seams kept visible in places for decorative purpose.
Purchase
Marks: Sidsel Dorph-Jensen, London
Small vessel: height 10.8cm · width 7cm
Medium vessel: height 15.7cm · width 8.5cm
Large vessel: height 21.9cm · width 8.7cm

Three vessels with indented sides as hand grips. Part of Sidsel Dorph-Jensen's 'liquid volume' series exploring new forms communicating a purpose; in this case the containing and pouring of liquids such as water and cream.

Born in Denmark in 1973. Master's degree, Royal College of Art, 2003.

Winner of the Goldsmiths' Company's 'Young Designer Silversmith Award', 2002.

Senior Fellow Bishopsland Educational Trust

Sidsel Dorph-Jensen uses traditional silversmithing techniques unconventionally to allow reinterpretations of three-dimensional vessels. Her Danish and British silversmith training combine visually in her trans-cultural designs. Her work in silver is characteristically Danish in their finished surfaces but markedly British in their original artistic concept. Although her studio workshop is in Denmark, Sidsel frequently visits the UK.

Public Collections include:
2002 Fish Slice, The Rabinovitch Collection at the Victoria and Albert Museum, London;
2003 Vessels, the Victoria and Albert Museum, London;
2003 Pouring Vessel, Millenium Gallery, Museums, Sheffield;
2003 Vessels, Koldinghus Museum, Denmark;
2006 'Cherry' Bowl and Pouring Vessel, Fitzwilliam Museum, Cambridge;
2006 Finger Bowl, New College, Oxford.

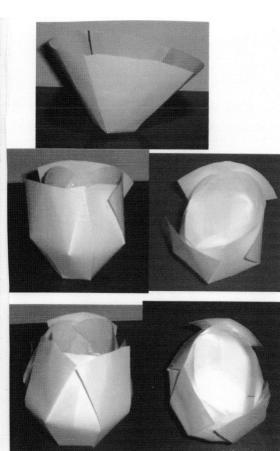

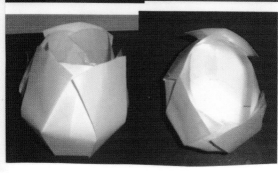

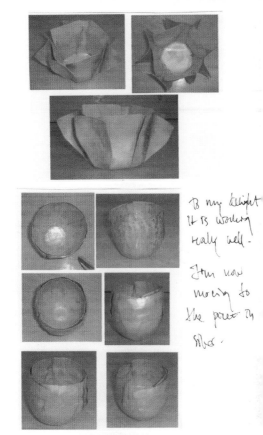

Sketchbook pages

THREE 'CUT-EDGE' VESSELS, 2006

Britannia silver. Using one sheet of silver, pierced sections are soldered together before hand-raising.
Commission
Marks: Sidsel Dorph-Jensen, London
Small vessel: height 8.7cm · diameter 9.4cm
Medium vessel: height 9.8cm · diameter 10.5cm
Large vessel: height 12.9cm · diameter 9.5cm

These vessels were commissioned following the exhibition of her new work in the 2006 'Collect' show on the Bishopsland Educational Trust stand at the Victoria and Albert Museum. The brief was to suggest the opening of a cabbage rose.

NDIDI EKUBIA

'My artistic landscape has been determined by the bold African shapes, textiles, food and passionate family conversation of my childhood. I am excited by the sensual and rich forms that can be created in metal and believe my nature is reflected through my work. It is a delight to be absorbed in every stage from design to the finished piece. Each piece exposes an emotional response to the material, each one a unique blend of order and chaos.'

Born 1973. Master's degree, the Royal College of Art, 1998. Bishopsland Educational Trust Fellow 1995–96, Senior Fellow Bishopsland Educational Trust.

Of Nigerian descent, Ndidi Ekubia has made hand-raising her own exuberant speciality, which gives her hammered silver pieces a sensual and rhythmic quality. Her studio workshop is in London.

Public Collections include:
2000 Bowl and Spoon, National Museum Wales, Cardiff;
2003 'Butterfly' Vase, Shipley Art Gallery, Gateshead;
2006 'Quiver' Vase, City Museum and Art Gallery, Bristol;
2006 Dish, Aberdeen Art Gallery and Museums;
2010 Large Bowl, Ashmolean Museum, Oxford;
2013 Vase, the Victoria and Albert Museum, London.

Selected Commissions include:
1997 Ablutions Bowl and Jug, Winchester Cathedral;
2012 Rosewater Dishes, The Worshipful Company of Weavers, London;
2009 Salver and Pair of Large Vases, The Worshipful Company of Grocers, London.

WINE COOLER, 2007

Britannia silver, hand-raised, with hammered decoration using different hammers and wooden stakes, creating organic patterns which gives this functional vessel a sense of fluidity and movement.
Commission
Marks: Ndidi Ekubia, London
Height 20cm · diameter 28.3cm

This was Ndidi Ekubia's first commission for the Goldsmiths' Company.

BEAKER, 2013

Britannia silver. Hand-raised, with hammered decoration.
Purchase
Marks: Ndidi Ekubia, London
Height 8.5cm · diameter 7.5cm

The beaker was purchased from the 'Bishopsland Contemporary Silver' exhibition, Drapers' Hall, London, 2014.

RICHARD FOX

'I relish the opportunity to design for well-known establishments such as trophy work for Formula One, ecumenical silver for Lambeth Palace, working with Rolls Royce Motor Cars on their bespoke car interiors and exteriors, Pernod Ricard on exclusive bottles of very rare whisky, Architects, Fashion Designers, Museums, Films and The Silver Trust for Downing Street. I like to design silver items that are useable, whilst retaining their elegance.'

Born 1954. Master's degree, Royal College of Art, 1981. Chairman of the Contemporary British Silversmiths 1999–2002. Current Treasurer of Contemporary British Silversmiths. Member of the Court of Assistants of the Goldsmiths' Company since 2011. Current Chairman of the Goldsmiths' Centre Working Group and Current Chairman of the Goldsmiths' Company Antique Plate Committee.

Richard Fox runs a contemporary design-led silver manufacturing company in London with his wife, Serena, herself a jeweller, employing eight craftsmen, concentrating on limited batch production of silver items. He specialises in motor racing trophies, corporate gifts and domestic silver; however, he also undertakes one-off silver commissions for ecclesiastical and other patrons.

Selected Commissions include:
1984 The Bernie Ecclestone Trophy and Formula One TV Trophy;
1991 Chalice and Paten, Lichfield Cathedral;
1992 Chalice, Gift from His Grace The Archbishop of Canterbury to His Holiness Pope John Paul II;
1995 Cruet Sets, The Silver Trust for No.10 Downing Street, London;
1995–2015 Formula One Championship Driver and Constructors Trophies, World Rally Drivers' and Manufacturers' Trophies;
1997 Hanging Pyx, Norwich Cathedral;
1998 Ciborium, Selby Abbey;
1999 Crozier, Pectoral Cross, and Bishop's Ring, for John Sentamu, Bishop of Stepney, London;
2001 Pair of Candelabra, The Worshipful Company of Information Technologists, London;
2004 'Principa' Table Fountain, (collaboration with Angela Connor), The Silver Trust for No.10 Downing Street, London;
2005 Pectoral Cross Gift from His Grace The Archbishop of Canterbury to His Holiness Pope Benedict;
2006 Loving Cup, The Worshipful Company of Information Technologists, London;
2011 Bed Side Table Lamps, Bulgari Hotel, Knightsbridge;
2012 'Magnolia' Dish, for Michael Galsworthy, past Prime Warden of the Worshipful Company of Goldsmiths;

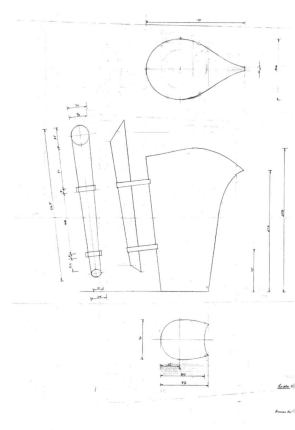

Design drawing

2013 'Celestial' bespoke interior for Rolls Royce Phantom;
2014 'Yas Marina Perpetual' Trophy, Abu Dhabi;
2015 Glenlivet 50 Year Old Project, Chivas Brothers.

The Goldsmiths' Company Modern Silver Collection (not included in the exhibition):
1984 Pair of Four Light Candelabra;
1993 Saint Dunstan Chalice.

'RIVIERA' JUG, 2008

Fabricated, seamed, with computer engraved fluted spout. Turned tulip wood handle. Designed for production.
Commission
Marks: Richard Fox, London
Height 27.5cm · width 25cm

'In 2007 Contemporary British Silversmiths held an International Symposium at Aston University in Birmingham called CONNECT. As part of the event it was decided to ask the members to create a new piece of work on the theme of dining in response to one of two objects: a simple white porcelain bowl, designed by Jasper Conran and manufactured by Wedgwood, and a more ornate, cut and etched crystal glass manufactured by Tudor Crystal. Cookson Precious metals provided up to a kilo of silver for each of the 40 participating silversmiths.

I chose the Tudor Crystal glass which had ornate glass engravings of flowers on the sides and a star burst engraved into the base. I wanted to create a design which contrasted between the highly decorative finish of the glass and the bold form of the jug. The star burst detail was carried through into the computer engraved flutes that cut through the body creating the spout which, in contrast to the highly polished body, is matt finished. The form is a 'simple' wrap from a rectangular sheet of silver with the flutes cutting through the wrap to create the spout. The inside of the jug is 24ct hard gold plated and the jug has a tulip wood handle. Whether for Champagne or for Pimms, the design required a name synonymous with elegance hence – "Riviera".'
Richard Fox, 2015

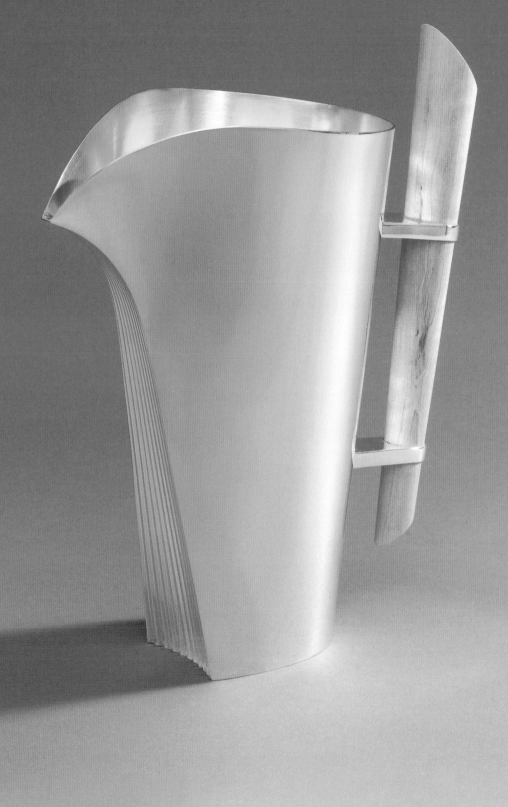

KEVIN GREY

'During my studies the simplicity of 20th century Scandinavian design appealed to me – and these forms became the starting point to developing my own work. The work I now produce comes from this tradition and a responsive aptitude to making. The processes I use couple traditional metalworking skills with new technology – in particular laser and TIG welding. Individual strips of silver are hand-formed before being joined to form a complex surface. A number of surface elements within one piece can collide to create contrasting smooth and jagged edges, resulting in decorative qualities and surface depth. The volumes that the final pieces take are visualized at the outset – but the surface quality and resulting jagged edges emerge as the work is made.'

Born 1967. Formerly worked in the automotive industry, producing hand-made bespoke pieces for Rolls Royce and Bentley. Kevin later worked for Morgan Motor Company but changed career to silversmithing

in 2007. Graduated Birmingham School of Jewellery 2009. Two years of Artist in Residence at the Birmingham School of Jewellery. Senior Fellow Bishopsland Educational Trust. Won the Goldsmiths' Company Award in 2010, 2012 and 2014.

Kevin Grey's silver work uses Laser and TIG welding in a highly original way which he produces in his Birmingham studio workshop.

Public Collections include:
2011 'Filiere' Bowl, Birmingham Museum and Art Gallery, Museum of the Jewellery Quarter;
2011 'Fractured' sculptural object, P&O Makower Silver Trust donated to the National Museum of Wales, Cardiff.

'SINEW' VESSEL, 2011

Britannia silver, circular central bowl with three outer walls formed of overlapping strips. Hand-shaped strips, laser welded together and soldered to hand-raised inner.
Commission
Marks: Kevin Grey, Birmingham
Height 9.3cm · width 11cm

Commissioned as a result of the work on his stand at Goldsmiths' Fair 2010. Kevin Grey's brief was to evoke the overlay of muscles in the human body in a silver vessel form. He was instructed to visit The Wellcome Collection in London to view such material before presenting his design to the Goldsmiths' Company's Modern Collection Committee.

This commission was in response to a similar piece seen at 'British Silver Week', 2011.

MIRIAM HANID

'The fluidity and movement of flowing water inspires my "painting in metal".

The inspiration comes from the imagery of water, particularly the sea. I see water as a metaphor for the divine current of energy flowing through all forms of life. I record the ever changing element of water in drawings and photographs. Rough sketches then inform the silver framework but the silver form then changes rapidly throughout the making process'.

Born 1986. Graduated from University of the Creative Arts Farnham, 2007. Bishopsland Educational Trust Fellow 2007–2008. Senior Fellow of the Bishopsland Educational Trust. Artist in residence for The Goldsmiths' Company 'Studio Silver Today' exhibition series, at Ickworth House, Suffolk, in liaison with The National Trust, 2012.

Miriam Hanid uses the silversmithing techniques of raising, chasing, repoussé chasing and hand-engraving in a particularly fluid manner. Her studio workshop is in Suffolk, by the sea.

Public Collections include:
2010 'Coriolis' Centrepiece, P&O Makower Trust on loan to the National Museum Wales, Cardiff;
2013 'Union' Centrepiece, the Victoria and Albert Museum, London.

Selected Commissions include:
2012 Diamond Jubilee Engraved Band for HM The Queen, The Worshipful Company of Drapers, London;
2012 Water Beaker, New College, Oxford.

Miriam Hanid photographing the sea

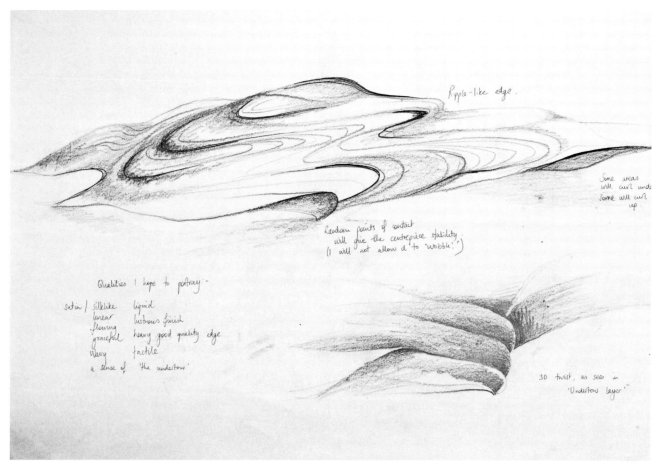

Ripple-like edge.

Some areas
will curl under
some will curl
up.

Random points of contact
will give the centrepiece stability.
(I will not allow it to 'wobble'.)

Qualities I hope to portray:-

satin / silklike   liquid
linear   lustrous finish
flowing   heavy good quality edge
graceful
wavy   tactile
a sense of 'the undertow'

3D twist, as seen in
'Undertow layer'

Drawings

'DELUGE' DISH, 2009

Fine silver. Hand repoussé chased and formed on wood using wooden hammers, to preserve the soft surface quality of the fine silver, with subtle engraved decoration.
Commission
Marks: Miriam Hanid, London
Height 11cm · length 67cm · width 33cm

Inspired by the imagery of water, Miriam Hanid uses the momentary pattern in flowing water as her starting point. This centrepiece evokes the ebb and flow of Atlantic waves breaking on the coast.

Commissioned as a result of Miriam's first wave dish that she made for the renowned artist cabinet maker, John Makepeace, who uses it to display different olives for pre-drinks for his guests.

'RIPPLE' BEAKER, 2010

Part spun and hand-raised form, planished, chased and hammer chased.
Purchase
Marks: Miriam Hanid, London
Height 7.6cm · width 7.7cm

The chased flowing lines and ripples were taken from sketches of reflections in a stream running through some woods. The satin finish on the beaker is soft when held in the hand, like the flow of water around one's hand when placed in a flowing stream. The beaker was purchased following the 'British Silver Week' exhibition, 2012.

'SEA BIRDS IN FLIGHT' VASE, 2013

Britannia Silver. Formed, chased, hand-engraved and chiselled, part gilt.
Commission
Marks: Miriam Hanid, London
Height 15cm · diameter 16.5cm

Commissioned to evoke the seasonal flight passage of birds around the world, Miriam researched cloud types, such as stratus, cumulus, cumulonimbus, in order to plan the clouds on the circular form. Clouds and wavy seas form the backdrop to a swirling flutter of birds. The chased, engraved and carved birds in flight and sea waves are enhanced by subtle chased lines, indicating the ocean winds. Craftsmanship is used here sensitively and innovatively to realise the narrative.

WATER JUG, 2015

Fine Silver. Formed, chased and planished.
Commission
Marks: Miriam Hanid, London
Height 18cm · width 25cm · depth 18cm

'The inspiration for the chasing and
forming which characterise this jug
stems from the movement of water
inside it. The way the water might move
around when being poured into and out
of the jug seemed a natural starting point
on which to base a lineal pattern. The
undulating chasing blends from wider
valleys to crisper lines, thus capturing
movement within and around the form.
The finely planished (hammered) surface
gives a shimmering quality rather like
that of sun on the softly moving sea.
From inspiration to usage, this piece is
made to capture water!'
Miriam Hanid 2015

RAUNI HIGSON

'I experiment a lot in copper, making models and prototypes. Experience means the results become more predictable, and pitfalls are more avoidable, but the planning process doesn't have an end point before making begins. I respond to the piece as I'm forming it, hammering intuitively. Fold-forming results in an imperfect symmetry which is very common in nature. The forms that emerge are often reminiscent of growth patterns found in plants, fungi, corals and shells. I love the aesthetic results, the really strong, lightweight structures, but also the magic moment of the "reveal" at the end.'

PAIR OF 'UNFURL' NAPKIN RINGS, 2003

Creased and hammered in thin gauge silver. V-shaped silver strips in open-ended spiral forms, which are textured.
Purchase
Marks: Rauni Higson, London
Height 7cm · diameter 7.2cm

These napkin rings were purchased in 2003 from The Metal Gallery, owned by Francis Raeymaekers, in Mount Street, London, now closed.

Born 1970. Trained at Lahti Design Institute, Finland. Graduate of the University of Central England, Birmingham 1996. Artist in residence for the Goldsmiths' Company's 'Studio Silver Today' exhibition series, at Erddig Hall, Wrexham, in liaison with The National Trust, 2013. Currently Chair of Contemporary British Silversmiths. Her studio workshop is in North Wales.

Rauni Higson combines traditional hammer skills with a creasing technique called fold-forming. A sheet of metal is folded completely flat, like folding a piece of paper, hammered whilst folded which distorts it considerably, and then opened out into the final 3D form which varies according to the hammering.

Public Collections include:
2015 'Glacier II', National Museum of Wales, Cardiff.

Selected Commissions include:
2003 Episcopal Ring and Pectoral Cross, The Bishop of St David's;
2004 Communion Set and Pair of Altar Candlesticks, St. Catherine's Church, Pontypridd;
2004 Centenary Trophy, The Welsh Ladies Golf Union;
2009 'Undersea' Candelabra, Aspreys, London;
2010 'Eucalyptus' Cutlery (2 settings), Margo Grant Walsh Collection, part of the collection published as 'Collecting by Design', USA;
2011 Dish, Royal Wedding gift for the Duke and Duchess of Cambridge. Commissioned on behalf of the People of the Royal County of Berkshire, by the Lord-Lieutenant of the county;
2015 Loving Cup, The Worshipful Company of Clothworkers, London.

'IRIS' SALVER, 2009

Flat hammered with a sunk well and 17 fold-formed elements soldered to the rim.
Commission
Marks: Rauni Higson, London
Diameter 30cm

Commissioned as a second version of a salver, that was originally commissioned by Francis Raeymaekers. Rauni Higson worked on the original salver under the tutoring of the renowned silver craftsman, Christopher Lawrence, using the old fashioned technique of flat hammering. The technique of soldering the 17 fold form elements around the rim was deliberate, in order that the back of the rim was smooth and the piece had thickness and weight to it. This Goldsmiths' Company's salver directly inspired a further similar commission for Rauni Higson, of a wedding gift to the Duke and Duchess of Cambridge in 2011.

'EUCALYPTUS' CUTLERY SET, 2011

Hand-forged silver with steel knife blades.
Commission
Marks: Rauni Higson, London
Large knife: length 23cm · width 2.5cm
Small knife: length 20.5cm · width 2.3cm
Large fork: length 20.5cm · width 3cm
Small fork: length 18cm · width 2.8cm
Fruit spoon: length 20cm · width 4cm
Dessert spoon: length 14.5cm · width 3cm
Teaspoon: length 17cm · width 3.3cm

An example of Rauni Higson's innovative cutlery design originally made as a sample setting, exhibited at the Metal Gallery, London.

Drawings

'PERSEPHONE' VASE, 2012

Britannia Silver. Spun and hand-raised vase,
with soldered fold-formed elements.
Commission
Marks: Rauni Higson, London
Height 54.5cm · width 25cm

The myth of Persephone's abduction
by Hades represents her function
as the personification of vegetation
which shoots forth in Spring and
withdraws into the earth after harvest.

   This vase represents the
irrepressible growth of Spring;
inspired by the Snowdonia landscape
where plants strive against the hard
mountain elements, emerging from
cracks and fissures with immense
energy. Commissioned as the
centrepiece of her showcase silver
exhibits at Erddig Hall, when she was
artist in residence for the Goldsmiths'
Company's 'Studio Silver Today'
exhibition, in liaison with the
National Trust, 2013.

'GLACIER' DISH, 2013

Hammer-formed, using a selection of stakes and formers, many custom-made, and adapted hammers. The main body of the piece was formed from a single sheet, which then had a segment removed. This was replaced by the flowing element, asymmetrically bisecting the smooth form.
Purchase
Marks: Rauni Higson, London
length 37cm · width 20.5cm

The aim of this piece was to capture the movement and flow in the seemingly unyielding medium of metal to convey the overwhelming power of glaciers carving landscapes out of solid rock. The exceptional finely tuned free-form hammering displayed within the piece was the result of Rauni's week internship with the artist-chaser Michael Lloyd in Scotland.

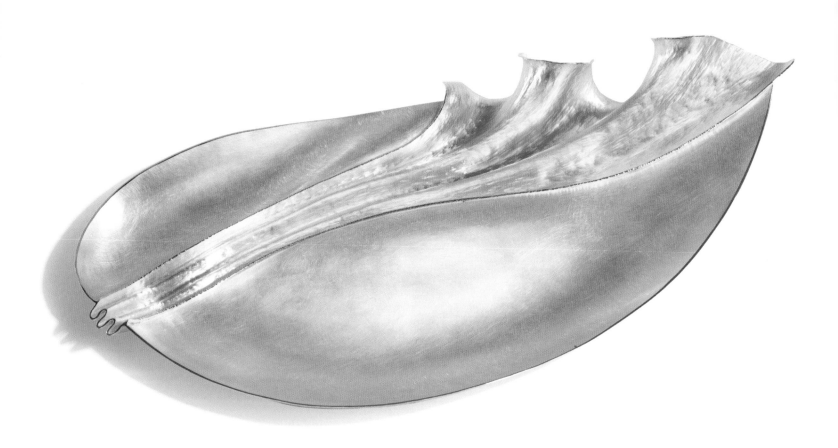

'MOUNTAIN BURN' ROSEWATER DISH, 2015

Formed by spinning, hand-raised and flat-hammered. 'Water' element fabricated from 12 parts, hammered freehand using a selection of stakes and formers, this element is then soldered onto the dish.
Commission
Marks: Rauni Higson, London
Height 7cm · diameter 49cm

Commissioned to commemorate the year of office of Lord Sutherland as Prime Warden of the Goldsmiths' Company, 2012–13. The Dish is designed to capture the feeling and motion of water cascading down a Scottish burn, to evoke the landscape where Lord Sutherland lives. Silver is the perfect material to evoke water, reflective and responsive to light.

The 'burn' carves through and flows over the body of the dish. It will be used as part of the new Buffet Plate Display in the Livery Hall of the Goldsmiths' Company.

KATHRYN HINTON

Born 1981. Graduate of Jewellery and Silversmithing design, Kent Institute of Art and Design, 2003. Master's degree, Royal College of Art, 2008. Post-graduate residency, Bishopsland Educational Trust Fellow 2003–2004. Research student, Royal College of Art 2008–2010. Kathryn's studio workshop is in Edinburgh.

Kathryn Hinton's work focuses on merging traditional techniques with digital technology. The faceted forms are achieved by using computer aided design software, and realised through rapid prototyping. Computer Numerically Controlled (CNC) milling, casting and press forming.

The process provides a new layer of interaction between the hand and digital technologies.

Public Collections include:
2010 Faceted Cast Small Bowl, Crafts Council Collection.

Selected Commissions include:
2011 'Exhausted' Water Jug, Aberdeen Medico-Chirurgical Society.

'I have always been interested in the traditional methods of making and in learning the skills involved in different hand processes, but also in the possibilities and processes associated with computer aided design and new technologies. These interests have inspired the research I have undertaken at the Royal College of Art into digital tooling and the idea of merging traditional silversmithing processes with new technologies.'

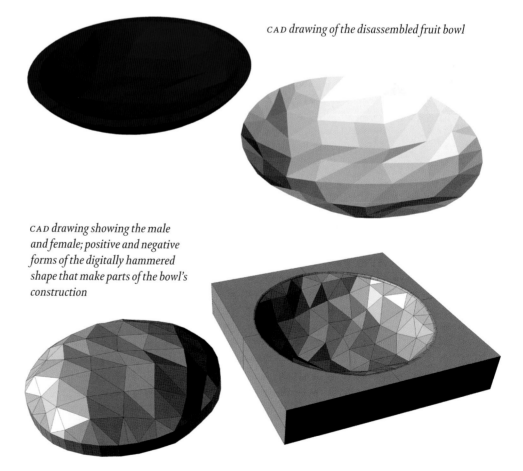

CAD *drawing of the disassembled fruit bowl*

CAD *drawing showing the male and female; positive and negative forms of the digitally hammered shape that make parts of the bowl's construction*

FRUIT BOWL, 2013

Faceted bowl on faceted purple heart wooden base.
Purchase
Marks: Kathryn Hinton, London
Silver fruit bowl: height 3.5cm · diameter 22.8cm
Wooden base: height 4.5cm · diameter 24.8cm

Focusing on merging traditional techniques with digital technology, Kathryn Hinton has developed here a user interface in the form of a hammer that works alongside computer aided design software to mimic the physical actions of silversmithing, in particular the hammering process used in forming sheet metal. The sterling silver and purple heart wooden fruit bowl was designed using the digital hammer and computer aided design software.

The digital file was used to make a press forming mould using computer numerically controlled (CNC) milling into which the silver sheet was pressed. The wooden bowl was wood turned and CNC-milled to achieve the faceted surface that the silver bowl fits in.

ADRIAN HOPE

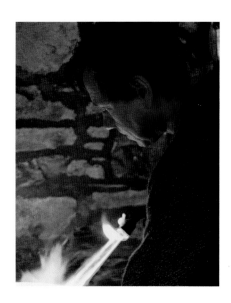

'Preciousness is a hindrance.
Usefulness a happy bonus.

    *I grew up in a house where both my
parents and my grandfather made things.
Broken things were repaired long before
replacement was even considered. Useful
things were always kept. My grandfather,
a civil engineer, took up furniture making.
A little chest of drawers for tools, a fishing
rod transport case, a book case. My father,
an architect, drew and painted, and made
models and a standard lamp out of spare
parts from a Spitfire.*

    *My mother took her cue from these
two men and she too made furniture. My
brother's interest lay in the theatre but
that too was definitely creative. For me
Art College would be almost impossible to
avoid. The foundation course in Brighton
allowed a student to try various fields and
one day, annealing a piece of gilding metal,
with a huge foot-bellowed torch, I was
seduced into becoming a silversmith.'*

Born 1953. Graduate of Edinburgh
College of Art 1977. Adrian's studio
workshop is in Scotland.

Adrian Hope spent a week working
with Mogens in Copenhagen in 1995,
learning a different way to raise silver.
His vessels are lightly hammered,
almost in the Arts and Crafts manner,
and are often decorated using paper
impressing and embossing.

Public Collections include:
1984 Coffee Pot and Candlesticks,
National Museums Scotland,
Edinburgh;
1988 Caddy, Bristol City Museum and
Art Gallery;
1990 Rocking Vessel, Kelvingrove
Museum and Art Gallery Glasgow;
1993 Coffee Pot, Box and Candlesticks,
Aberdeen Art Gallery, Scotland;
1995 Fish Server, The Rabinovitch
Collection at the Victoria and Albert
Museum, London;
2003 Reliquary, Birmingham Museum
and Art Gallery;
2008 Plate, National Museums
Scotland, Edinburgh.

Selected Commissions include:
1999 Twenty-Six Cutlery Place Settings,
the Incorporation of Goldsmiths,
Edinburgh, loaned to Bute House,
Edinburgh;
2002 Rosewater Bowl, The Worshipful
Company of Haberdashers, London;
2002 King George VI and Queen
Elizabeth Diamond Stakes Trophy for
De Beers, Ascot;
2010 Reliquary, The Pearson Collection;
2014 'Holly' Teapot, The
Pearson Collection.

*The Goldsmiths' Company Modern Silver
Collection (not included in the exhibition):*
1992 Dish

TWO PLATES, 2005

Britannia silver. Embossed with a paper impressed design. Using wooden mallets, punches and formers, the plates are embossed and sunk.
Purchase
Marks: Adrian Hope, London
Plate 1: Diameter 28 cm
Plate 2: Diameter 27.8cm

BOWL, 2005

Britannia silver. Hand-raised shallow bowl with paper impressed design.
Purchase
Marks: Adrian Hope, London
Height 5cm · diameter 15.5cm

A new development in Adrian Hope's work: he uses large rollers initially to imprint the paper design onto the silver.

'SNOW' BOWL, 2009

Britannia Silver. Hand-raised using wooden stakes and a wooden mallet with ripple effect, hammered texture.
Purchase
Marks: Adrian Hope, London
Height 17.5cm · diameter 13.5cm

'People watch the raising process and they see a person hammering away. The assumption almost always seems to be that the metal is being stretched. It is, quite remarkably, being compressed.' Adrian Hope 2014.

This piece was originally exhibited at Goldsmiths' Fair 2009.

'SNOWCORD' VASE, 2010

Britannia silver. Hand-raised using wooden stakes and a wooden mallet, hammered textured matt finish with stone and engraved comb effect.
Purchase
Marks: Adrian Hope, London
Height 17.5cm · diameter 13.5cm

Inspired by the 'Kingdom of the Ife' exhibition (early bronze workers) at The British Museum, this piece was purchased through 'Origin'.

The softness of the silver finish is only achieved by the use of wooden tools. The intent was to make an object as direct as possible, as simple as drawing an outline sketch. The immediacy of the making of this bowl is akin to the immediacy of making a snowball.

VASE, 2014

Commission
Marks: Adrian Hope, London
Height 24.3 cm · diameter 11.5 cm

This vase is the result of a new method of production by Adrian Hope:

'I have been working on prototypes for a swaging engine. This has been a slow process and while nothing under development can be called finished the latest version is an effective device…
I adjust the device, I turn the handle. The line or flute is there in seconds. With it I can emboss flutes, everted and inverted into the wall of a vessel. I can steer these lines. I can make them hard and sharp, or soft and swelling.

I can start and stop the movement anywhere. I can do all this on a vertical axis or a radial axis. I can bouge the surface, i.e. a swelling or indentation with or without a hard boundary. Two arms each support shaped wheels. Depending on the chosen function the wheel might be steel, nylon or delrin. The arm ends can be pressured against each other, aligned on different axes and adjusted to cope with different curves in the vessels worked on.'

Adrian Hope, 2014.

KYOSUN JUNG

'I studied Metal Craft and Jewellery in Korea for two years before I came to study in the UK. To start with, I was more interested in jewellery. However, in my second year I won the Young Designer Silversmith Award and was given the opportunity to make my Sake Set at The Goldsmiths' Centre in Clive Burr's workshop. I really enjoyed the whole development, from refining my design, the making process, to completing the final piece. It was just amazing, and I decided I wanted to become a silversmith. I draw inspiration from nature and organic forms; their infinite creations, patterns and textures. I like to look at new processes to take inspiration, always challenging myself. I consider it very important to explore new technologies in design and craft manufacturing; to me this is essential in the process. My desire is also to challenge conventions and perceptions. I hope that the pieces that I have developed and created so far can be admired for their visual beauty as well as the intended function and purpose.'

Born in South Korea in 1984. Graduate of Jangan College, Korea, 2006 and the University for the Creative Arts in Rochester, 2014. The Goldsmiths' Company 'Young Designer Silversmith Award', 2013. Kyosun's studio workshop is in London.

Kyosun combines Oriental and European aesthetics in her designs. These begin as free-hand drawings and then are transferred by her into Proficient Computer Aided Designs for fabrication accuracy, where she will use both hand and machine technical skills to realise the concept.

Public Collections include:
2013 Sake Set, the Victoria and Albert Museum, London.

Selected Commissions include:
2014 'Ivory Exploitation' Bronze Medal, Harrow School, London.

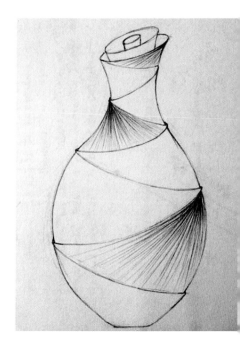

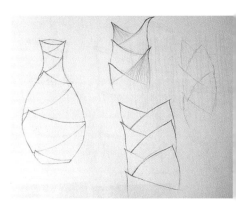

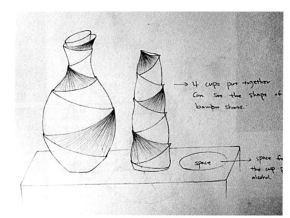

Drawings

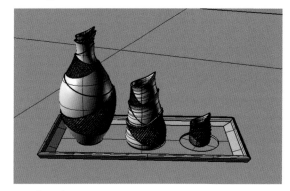

CAD Drawing

Rapid prototype model

'SAKE' DRINKING SET, 2015

Spun, fabricated and engraved, with multiple separate wires, individually soldered. On bamboo and African wenge tray.
Commission
Marks: Kyosun Jung, London
Bottle: height 19cm · diameter 10cm
Cup 1: height 6cm · diameter 7. 1cm
Cup 2: height 5.9cm · diameter 5.9cm
Cup 3: height 5.8cm · diameter 4. 9cm
Cup 4: height 5.6cm · diameter 3.9cm
Tray: height 20 cm · width 38 cm ·depth 2 cm

This set was commissioned to replicate Kyosun's piece entered in 2013 to the Goldsmiths' Company's 'Young Designer Silversmith Award'. The 'Young Designer Silversmith Award' was a prestigious award given by the Goldsmiths' Company between 1994 and 2013. The award encouraged contemporary studio silver design and dexterity of craftsmanship. It took the form of a design competition aimed at silversmithing students, the winner being mentored in a major silversmithing workshop to make up the piece. The finished piece was then presented to a national museum nearest to the student's college. In 2014 the award was replaced by a new initiative – Master Craftsman Internships, giving the opportunity to 20 silversmiths to extend their skills during internships with master craftsmen. The internships build upon the core aspect of the 'Young Designer Silversmiths Award', enabling students and mid-career silversmiths alike the opportunity to develop their skills in a particular area, often at critical moments in their career.

This commission commemorates the overall success of the prestigious 'Young Designer Silversmith Award'. Kyosun worked to the competition brief to design a drinking set for a particular spirit. After her design won the design competition in 2013, Kyosun was then mentored to make it up in silver in the workshop of Clive Burr, silversmith. The finished set was presented by the Goldsmiths' Company to the Victoria and Albert Museum for its permanent collection. The form of the Sake drinking set was inspired by the growth and formation of bamboo stems, which is seen in the layered sheets of silver. The drinking cups are designed to sit inside one another, and to sit with the flask on a bamboo and African wenge tray. Sake is Japanese rice wine. In Japanese Shinto wedding ceremonies, the bride and groom take turns sipping sake from three different bowls, each one larger than the one before. The tradition represents sharing joys and sorrows.

PETYA KAPRALOVA

Artist's photograph of Ribblehead viaduct

'I create sculptural pieces, tableware and desk accessories which play on the idea of an object as functional as it is sculptural. I work in combinations of pure iron and sterling silver exploring the high contrast of colour and tone between those two materials. The unexpected blues and purples in the dark iron provide the backdrop for the gentle silver image.

Every piece I create explores a specific landscape, location or situation in which I find a personal connection. I look for a sense of perspective, composition balance and storytelling through a single object. Each one of my pieces is unique and has its own narrative.'

Born in Bulgaria in 1986. Graduated from University for the Creative Arts, Farnham, 2009.

Petya Kapralova uses the traditional skills of hand-forging combined with the decorative technique of inlay, using a mixture of precious silver and non-precious iron. Her studio workshop is in Surrey.

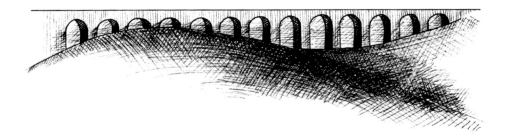

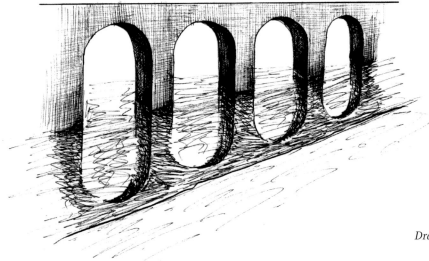

Drawings

'VIADUCT' CUTLERY SET, 2013

Hand-forged knife, fork and spoon in sterling silver, resting on a pure iron stand with silver inlay.
Purchase
Marks: Petya Kapralova, London
Knife: length 22.8cm · width 1.8cm
Fork: length 20.1cm · width 1.9cm
Spoon: height 21.5cm · width 1.9cm
Stand: height 25.5cm · width 6cm

The notion of different materials visually harmonising together inspired her composition balance when designing her pieces. Here she was inspired by the Ribblehead viaduct, an imposing engineered structure that cuts through the rolling North Yorkshire hills. Completed in 1874, the viaduct consists of 24 arches, composed of 1.5 million stone bricks, and was built to carry the Settle-Carlisle railway across the valley, and it is still in use. Petya Kapralova focused on the reality of the viaduct being subject in its design to the curves and irregularities of the landscape in which it sits. Her design for the knife, fork and spoon follow the curve of the base, just as the viaduct follows the landscape. The flat upper edge of the cutlery is designed to represent a train track. The inlay on the base mimics the viaduct arches and its reflection in the soft satin finish of the knife blade reaffirms the viaduct theme. When placed together on their base, the three pieces of cutlery fit within each other and are in fact almost hidden by the spoon. This design feature plays on the idea of a piece as being functional as well as sculptural. The function, though a vital part of the design, is not apparent and can remain a secret between the sculptor and viewer.

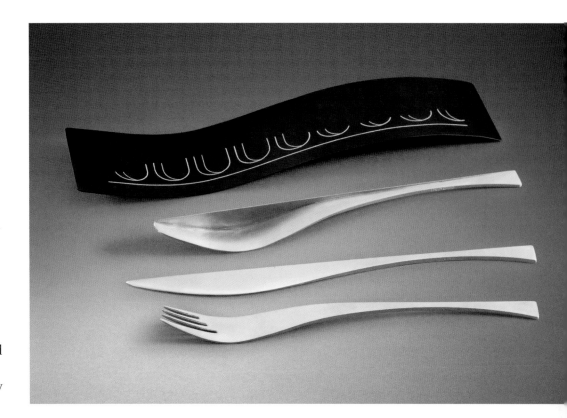

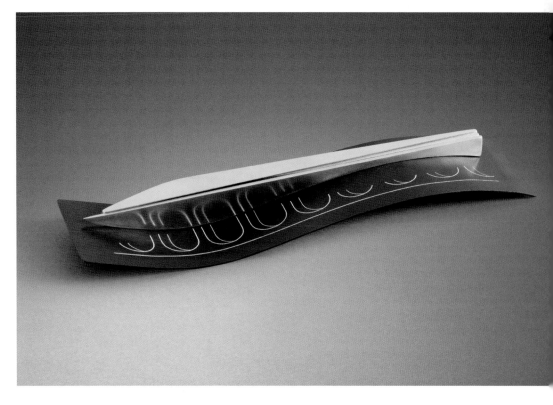

ROD KELLY

'Silver is a beautiful material to raise and chase, it responds perfectly and is a pleasure to use and form. I prefer to work around ideas and subjects initially suggested by clients; these are developed into commissioned pieces that then have a relevance and a closer relation to the individuals involved. I'll go anywhere to get a feel for my subject matter, whether it's a river to study wild brown trout, London Zoo to study leopards, or visiting historic buildings to draw and capture views and details, all of which are then woven into my designs.'

Born 1956. Graduate of Birmingham School of Silversmithing and Jewellery, 1979. Master's degree, Royal College of Art, 1983. Senior Fellow and Professor of Silver, Bishopsland Educational Trust. His studio workshops are in Norfolk and Shetland.

Rod Kelly hand-raises his design forms, specialising in low relief hand-chasing, interweaving narrative images related to a specific commission. All commissions start with a hand-drawn design.

Public Collections include:
1985 The Harvest Bowl, National Museums Scotland, Edinburgh;
1985 The 'Schumacher' Medal, The British Museum, London;
1990 Water Jug, Birmingham Museum and Art Gallery;
1996 The 'Black Thorn' Vase, Norwich Castle Museum, Norwich;
1996 Beaker, National Museums Scotland, Edinburgh;
1997 Cake Slice, The Rabinovitch Collection at the Victoria and Albert Museum, London;
2001 Vase, Norwich Castle Museum;
2003 Silver Book Binding Kelmscott Chaucer, Fitzwilliam Museum, Cambridge. (Believed to be the largest book ever bound in silver);
2005 Silver Binding Lectern Bible, commissioned by the Whitley Trust, the Victoria and Albert Museum, London;
2010 Dish and Ewer, Ashmolean Museum, Oxford.

Selected Commissions include:
1985 King George VI and Queen Elizabeth Diamond Stakes Racing Trophy, De Beers;
1988 Rose Bowl, Gift of the Victoria and Albert Museum to HM Queen Elizabeth The Queen Mother;
1990 Alms Dish, Lichfield Cathedral;
1990 Wine Cooler, gift to The Rt. Hon Edward Heath to commemorate his 40 years as a Member of Parliament;
1990 Rose Bowl, The Worshipful Company of Merchant Taylors, London as a gift to the late Diana, Princess of Wales when she was made a Freeman of the Company;
1992–3 Two Vases and Two Dishes, the Silver Trust for No.10 Downing Street, London;

1995 Processional Cross, The Grosvenor Chapel, Mayfair, London;
1996 Bishop's Crozier, Bishop of Stafford;
2000 Hanging Pyx, St Paul's Cathedral, London;
2000 Pair of Ciboria, York Minster;
2004 Tabernacle Doors, St John's Wood Church, London;
2006 Design for a Two Pound Coin celebrating the work of I.K. Brunel, The Royal Mint, London;
2007 Font, Leeds Catholic Cathedral;
2007 University Mace, Henley Management College;
2008 Altar Candlesticks, Durham Cathedral;
2008 The Golden Jubilee Stakes celebrating HM The Queen's Golden Jubilee, commissioned by the Duke of Devonshire for Ascot;
2009 Centrepiece, The Worshipful Company of Clothworkers, London;
2009 Chalice and Paten for the Abbot, St Louis Monastery, St Louis, Missouri, USA;
2011 Royal Wedding Present for the Royal Wedding of the Duke and Duchess of Cambridge, commissioned by the Royal Warrant Association;
2011 Altar Candlesticks for St Andrew's, Burton upon Stather, commissioned by Lady Inchyra;
2011 Loving Cup, The Guild of Weavers, Fullers and Shearmen , Tuckers' Hall, Exeter, Devon;
2013 Font, Holy Trinity, Salcombe, Devon;
2014 The Newton Oxford Cambridge Women's Boat Race Trophy, commissioned by Newton Bank;
2014 Low Mass Altar Candlesticks, St Alban's, Romford, Essex.

The Goldsmiths' Company Modern Silver Collection (*not included in the exhibition*):
1984 Four Goblets;
1985 Willow and Trout Water Jug;
1986 Amity Rosewater Dish and Ewer;
1989 Honeycombe Vase;
1997 Minorco Gold Bowl;
2015 Guest Goblet, gift to The Goldsmiths' Company of Elizabeth Rowe, in memory of Robert Rowe, Liveryman.

WINE COASTER, 2004 AND PORT LABEL, 2010

Hand-raised, hammered and chased in low relief with fine gold inlay and walnut base. Port label chased.
Commission
Marks: Rod Kelly, London
Coaster: height 10.3cm · diameter 14.7cm
Port Label: height 7.5cm · width 5.8cm

Six coasters for port decanter circulation at Livery Dinners at Goldsmiths' Hall were commissioned to commemorate Mr Richard Came's year of office as Prime Warden of the Goldsmiths' Company 2002–2003. Mr Came's love of trees and his pride in being Prime Warden of the Goldsmiths' Company is echoed in the leaf designs and the leopard's head, the hallmark of the London Assay Office, housed at Goldsmiths' Hall since 1478.

Coaster 1 is decorated with horse chestnut leaves, two leopards' heads and inlaid fine gold detail.

The six port labels are in the form of leopards' heads, with chased lettering 'PORT'. These hang around the neck of the port decanters.

WATER BEAKER, 2013

Hand-raised and chased. Gilt interior.
Gift of Mr Richard Agutter
Marks: Rod Kelly, London
Height 9cm · diameter 8cm

Commissioned as one of a pair of water
beakers by Mr Richard Agutter, Prime
Warden of the Goldsmiths' Company
2013–2014, for use by the Prime Warden
and his or her guest at Court and Livery
Dinners at Goldsmiths' Hall. The
silversmithing theme around the piece
relates to the design and making of the
beaker, with the imagery of a pencil,
divider, ruler, hammers and flames.
The image of the male leopard refers to
hallmarking, and charmingly the lady
leopard, with long eye lashes, refers
to the fact that today there are women
Court members.

Detail of 'The Diamond Jubilee' Dish, 2015, see overleaf

'THE DIAMOND JUBILEE' DISH 2015

Raised, beaten sunk by hand, and hammered into an octagonal form, chased decoration. Parcel gilt highlights.
Commission
Marks: Rod Kelly, London
Diameter 56cm

Commissioned to commemorate the Diamond Jubilee of the reign of Her Majesty Queen Elizabeth II. The centre is chased with the royal crown and the cipher EIIR, against a background of flowing lines, signifying water. Each of the four applied panels represent the flowers of the four nations of the United Kingdom; roses for England; thistles for Scotland; daffodils for Wales; and shamrocks for Northern Ireland. The four raised panels produce a cross and represent HM The Queen as Defender of the Faith. The central island boss amidst the water holds the four nations together.

The dish will form the centrepiece in a new display in 2015 of contemporary designed pieces by modern silversmiths.

This display will be used on formal occasions in the Livery Hall of Goldsmiths' Hall as the Buffet Plate to highlight to the guests dining there the Company's role as a major patron of modern silver and the exceptional quality of the silver work. On 9 July 2015, HM The Queen was shown this dish at Buckingham Palace at a private audience with the artist silversmith and two Goldsmith Company members.

Drawing

CHRIS KNIGHT

'Historically the vessel form was a vehicle to express and communicate something about the time and culture to which it belonged. My pieces carry on the tradition of commenting on society through a static vessel form. A lot of my work starts by deconstructing the basic object. I search for its prime function, its basic formal needs. From then on I start to reconstruct the object, exploring how to push a prime functional attribute. By combining base metal elements with silver I aim to visually devalue the precious and concentrate the viewer on meaning, rather than value of the object. It is important that I leave room for these objects to speak and maybe for others to comment.'

Born 1964. Master's degree, Royal College of Art, 1992. Senior Lecturer, Metalwork and Jewellery, Sheffield Hallam University. Senior Fellow Bishopsland Educational Trust.

Chris Knight employs digital technology to assist in the design development of initial ideas, which are transferred into manufacture drawings. Traditional silversmithing processes of raising, spinning, box work, and general fabrication techniques are often partnered with modern techniques of laser welding, CNC, photo mechanical etching, laser cutting and rapid prototype to realise his designs. His studio workshop is in Sheffield.

Public Collections include:
1998 Pair of Candelabra, the Victoria and Albert Museum, London;
2002 'Field of Silver', Birmingham City Museum & Art Gallery;
2006 Pair of Candelabra, Millennium Gallery, Museums Sheffield;
2006 Coffee Set, Aberdeen Art Gallery;
2007 Rocking Tea Set, Castle Museum, Norwich;
2010 'Lest We Forget' Chalice, Museums Sheffield;
2010 Candelabra, Ulster Museum, National Museums Northern Ireland.

Selected Commissions include:
1996 Chalice and Paten, St Patrick's Cathedral, New York;
1997 Server, The Rabinovitch Collection at the Victoria and Albert Museum, London;
2001 Processional Cross, Pascal Candle Stand, Altar Candle Sticks, St Augustine's Church, New York;
2001 Millennium Punchbowl, Sheffield Assay Office (in collaboration with Alex Brogden, Brett Payne and Keith Tyssen);
2005 Communion Set, New York (a collaboration with Maria Hanson);
2006 Mistress Cutler's Mace, The Company of Cutlers, Hallamshire, Sheffield (in collaboration with Owen Waterhouse);
2007 The St Leger Stakes Trophy (in collaboration with Sarah Denny and Owen Waterhouse);
2008 Chalice and Ciborium, Sheffield Cathedral;
2009 The Fish Public Artwork, St Helier, Jersey;
2009 Paten, Sheffield Cathedral;
2014 'Our Father' Mandorla for Felix Varela, Transfiguration Church, New York.

The Goldsmiths' Company Modern Silver Collection (not included in the exhibition):
1995 Pair of Candelabra

DRINKING SET, 2008, BY CHRIS KNIGHT WITH MARIA HANSON

Machine-made anodised blue aluminium tray using a laser cutting technique, with three pieces of Britannia silver with Keum-boo 23ct bonded gold overlay, matt finished. Hand-raised cups and sunk tray. Keum-boo is the ancient Korean gilding technique, which is a permanent diffusion bonding of fine gold foil onto silver, through heat and pressure.
Purchase
Marks: Chris Knight and Maria Hanson, London

Tray: height 2cm · length 51cm · width 28.6cm
Dish: height 3.5cm · diameter 18.2cm
Cup 1 (мн): height 8.3cm · diameter 7.6cm
Cup2 (ск): height 8.3cm · diameter 7.7cm

This husband and wife team extends the concept of the ceremony of drinking from a vessel, further emphasised, by the stark contrast of machine-made versus hand-made. One's conception of a beverage, and an occasion, is altered by the material of the vessel used; drinking coffee from a paper cup is a different experience from drinking wine from a silver chalice. The silver cups and dish sit upon an anodised aluminium tray, which is a symbolic extension of the domestic table but makes references to a ceremonial altar.

The need to place the cups back on the plate when not being drunk from establishes a sense of unity both with the piece itself and those using it, making a ceremony.

WILLIAM (SANG-HYEOB) LEE

'The reason why I became a silversmith is I like using hammers a lot. I think that a silversmith's personality becomes evident in his works and inevitably his style of hammering is heavily influenced by it.'

As a Korean-British artist silversmith, William transposes his inspiration from oriental traditional philosophy into his hammered, innovative forms and surfaces. With regard to this he says:

'My design concept is inspired by the power of natural energy in nature, falling water, air movement, temperature. My intention is to express the energy of the inside, the power of nature, the change of fluid by gravity, not controllable by humans.'

Born in South Korea in 1974. William Lee trained in Korea as a junior coppersmith with Jang Won Coppersmith Ltd. 1993–94 and then as a junior silversmith with Woo-No Silver Tableware Ltd. Coming to the United Kingdom in 2000 to do a foundation course in sculpture at Exeter College, William Lee completed his BA (Hons) degree in Silversmithing and Metal work at Camberwell College of Arts, 2004. In 2002 he was project maker with British sculptor, Antony Gormley, and in 2003 won the Worshipful Company of Goldsmiths' 'Young Designer Silversmith Award'.

Guest Fellow, Bishopsland Educational Trust.

Using the traditional process of hand-raising from one disc of silver, William Lee hand hammers ornamentation without addition or reduction to produce seamless vessels. His studio workshop is in London.

Public Collections include:
2003 Sporting Trophy, the Victoria and Albert Museum, London;
2007 Vase, Aberdeen Art Gallery.

Selected Commissions include:
2009 Vase, The Worshipful Company of Grocers, London;
2011 Rose Bowl, Pembroke College, Cambridge.

VASE, 2005

Hand-raised from a single sheet of Britannia silver with hammered textured surface. The form rises from a smaller circular base ballooning outwards towards the top and then curves inwards to a narrow opening at the top.
Purchase
Marks: William Lee, London
Height 37cm · width 22.5cm

Similar in form to Chinese porcelain vases of the Meiping form found in the K'ang-hsi period 1662–1722.

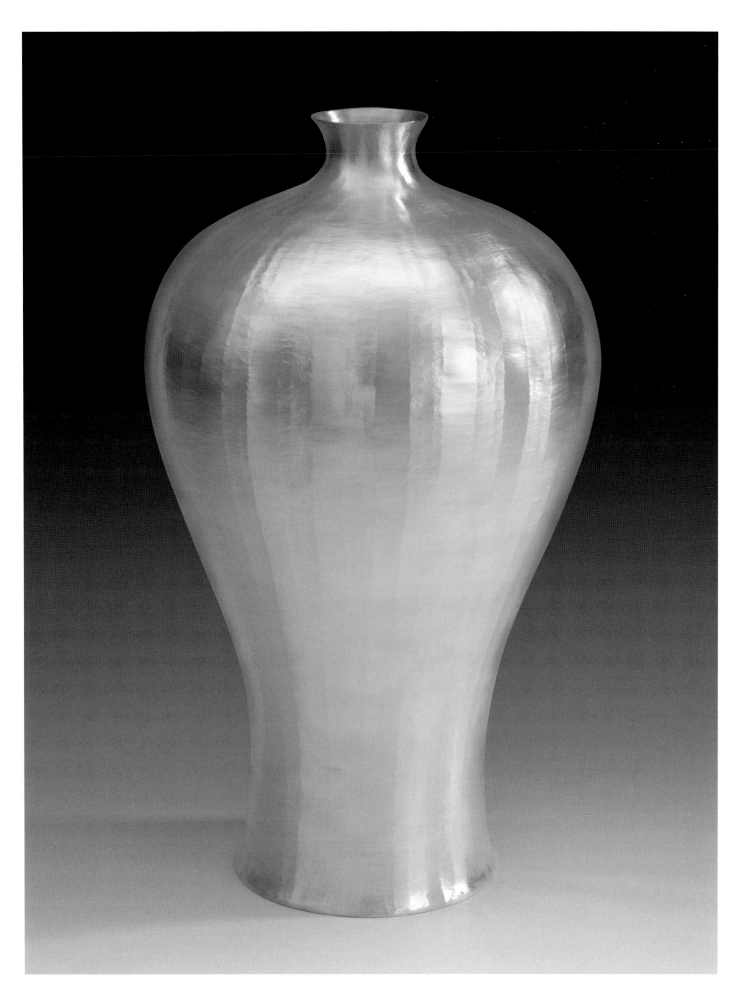

BEAKER, 2009

Fine silver. Tall beaker with slightly spiralling chasing. Hand-raised from single sheet of silver with hammered surface.
Purchase
Marks: William Lee, London
Height 10cm · diameter 7cm

BEAKER, 2009

Britannia silver. Chased line decoration. Hand-raised from single sheet of silver with hammered surface.
Purchase
Marks: William Lee, London
Height 7.8cm · diameter 8cm

BEAKER, 2010

Britannia silver. Hand-raised beaker, formed with flowing spiral hammer work.
Purchase
Marks: William Lee, London
Height 10.4cm · diameter 9cm

These beakers display the variety of shapes and surface treatments that William Lee achieves by just using hammers. His design inspiration begins with his experiments with falling liquids such as water, molten wax, honey and even tomato ketchup. From his observations of how gravity affects the shapes of these falling substances, he draws rough sketches of vessels 'attaching the idea' as he says to the overall design.

These beakers were purchased from Goldsmiths' Fair, 2009.

'MOON' VASE, 2010

Britannia silver, hand-raised vase with large spherical body with narrow flared neck and rim.
Purchase
Marks: William Lee, London
Height 33cm · diameter 33cm

The vase evokes the full moon and its ancient connecting spirituality to mankind. Its scale is a tour de force of skill of a single vessel being hand-raised from a single sheet of silver.

Purchased from Goldsmiths' Fair, 2010.

Detail of Vase

VASE, 2012

Fine silver, hand-raised vase.
Purchase
Marks: William Lee, London
Height 24.5cm · diameter 23cm

The concept is the observation of liquid to solid such as water freezing as it drops to form ice. Here the oriental connection to the potential that is found in the forces of nature is revered and celebrated in this vase. Purchased from Goldsmiths' Fair, 2012.

NAN NAN LIU

'I gained an interest in western media as a child from an advertisement I had seen on the television. I liked the sense of humour and the creative way of entertaining whilst cleverly promoting a product. I also enjoyed taking my mother's jewellery apart and then rebuilding it into my own design. As I got older I chose a typical path and went to university and studied accountancy but after one year I decided to do something different and came to England.

Looking at the rings within a tree shows the age of the tree but also a time in history. I started by making a collection of objects and accessories by building up layers in paper, and then in silver, using the idea of rings in a tree as my inspiration. I have gained a passion for working with metal in an organic way. I love the working progress, and after many hours of making layers I really enjoy seeing the interesting shapes and pattern created. I get the same joy through engraving, using a graver and cutting into the metal just like drawing with a pencil onto paper.'

Born in China in 1982. Graduate of Birmingham City University. Master's degree, Royal College of Art, 2010. Mentored in hand-engraving by Malcolm Appleby, artist-engraver, and by R H Wilkins, Hatton Garden, London in 2012. Senior Fellow and Tutor at Bishopsland Educational Trust 2007–2008.

Initially making intricate models in paper, Nan Nan specialises in fabricating and engraving. Her studio workshop is in North London.

Public Collections include:
2015 'Forrest' Sculptural Piece, P&O Makower Trust, loaned to the Victoria and Albert Museum, London.

Selected Commissions include:
2010 Lagoon Dish, John Higgins' Contemporary Silver Gallery.

'OYSTER' BOX, 2012

Britannia silver. Fabricated and hand-engraved. Commission
Marks: Nan Nan Liu, London
Height 4cm · length 14cm · width 9cm

Learning the skill of using the different cuts of traditional hand engraving from R H Wilkins in 2012 has influenced Nan Nan Liu's work here. The concept of this box is inspired by shells in seascapes and their connection to the forces of the natural world. The layers of silver flow around the box like sea water frozen, echoed in the subtle engraved patterns on the box lid.

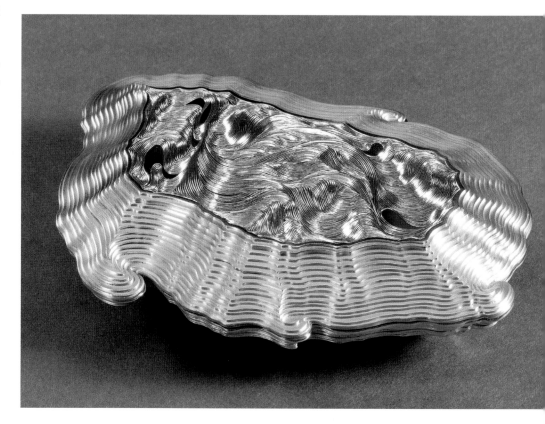

MICHAEL LLOYD

'I inhabit a very beautiful world, and I hope the work I make reflects my enjoyment and the profound sense of gratitude I feel from having made a livelihood from observing the nature of my surroundings. Work for me is a celebration of our creativity and of our environment; it is a homage to nature. If the finished piece marks a moment in time, a birth, a wedding, a memorable event, so much the better.'

Born 1950. Graduate of Birmingham School of Silversmithing and Jewellery. Master's degree, Royal College of Art, 1976.

Using the traditional silversmithing skills of hand-raising and hand-chasing, Michael Lloyd is inspired by the visual dictionary of the textures, forms and colours of the landscape of South West Scotland where he lives and works. His hand-drawn designs have a personal, spiritual content, reflecting his deep reverence for nature's beauty, charting the shapes of trees, leaves, flowers and fruit. Each silver piece is a direct response to something Michael has seen in the natural world. Making many drawings for one piece is his way of filtering images and distilling the silver design into a lyrical rhythm of pattern for chasing.

Public Collections include:
1975 Gold 'Corn' Bowl, the Victoria and Albert Museum, London;
1985 'Rush II' Bowl, Fitzwilliam Museum, Cambridge;
1987 'Beech' Bowl, Contemporary Art Society for Lincolnshire Museums;
1992 Cake Slice, The Rabinovitch Collection at the Victoria and Albert Museum, London;
1995 'Apple' Bowl, Shipley Art Gallery, Gateshead;
2000 Bowl, Aberdeen Art Gallery;
2002 Chalice and Two Dishes, National Museums Scotland, Edinburgh;
2004 'Spring' Vase, Birmingham Museum and Art Gallery;
2004 Gold 'Balcary Oak' Bowl, Birmingham Museum and Art Gallery;
2004 Clock, Birmingham Museum and Art Gallery;
2006 'Apple' Vase, Ashmolean Museum, Oxford.

Selected Commissions include:
1990 Processional Cross, The Church of St Francis, Sheffield (in collaboration with enameller Rosamond Conway);
1991 Offertory Salver, Lichfield Cathedral;
1992 Two Flower Bowls, The Silver Trust for No.10 Downing Street, London;
1993 Chalice, Carlisle Cathedral;
1993 The Sir Joseph Larmor Plate, St John's College, Cambridge;
1994 King George VI and Queen Elizabeth Diamond Stakes Trophy, De Beers, London;
1997 Two Fruit Dishes, The Silver Trust for No.10 Downing Street, London;
1999 Mace, HM The Queen for the Scottish Parliament, Edinburgh;
2000 Water Jugs, The Incorporation of Goldsmiths, Edinburgh and loaned to Bute House, Edinburgh;
2000 Four Chalices, York Minster;
2003 Two Chalices, Carlisle Cathedral;
2011 Processional Cross, St Albans, Romford;
2015 Chalice, Corpus Christie, Cambridge.

The Goldsmiths' Company Modern Silver Collection (not included in the exhibition):
1976 Two Bowls;
1985 Salver;
1990 Dish;
1994 Bowl;
1994 Dish.

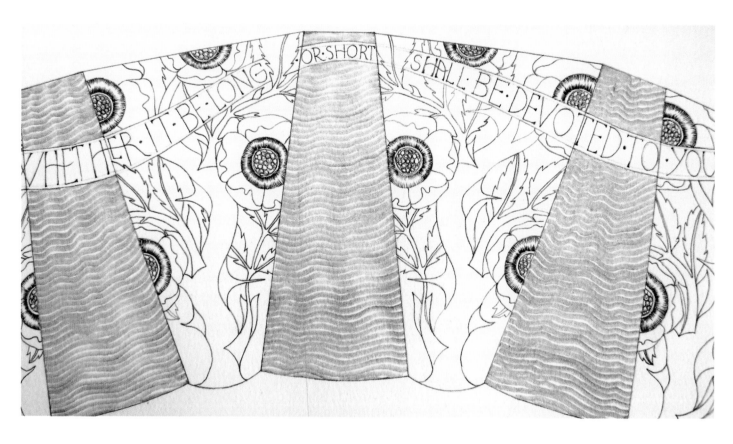

'THE JUBILEE BOWL', 2002

22 carat gold. Hand-raised, chased and engraved.
Commission
Marks: Michael Lloyd, Edinburgh
Height 15cm · diameter 14cm

Circular base rising to eight faceted panels. Alternating panels chased with Galloway roses and undulating lines. A banner with an inscription runs around the body. The inscription is taken from a speech made by the then Princess Elizabeth while on tour with her parents and sister in South Africa. The speech was made in radio broadcast to the Commonwealth on her 21st birthday (21st April 1947).

Inscription: "MY WHOLE LIFE WHETHER IT BE LONG OR SHORT SHALL BE DEVOTED TO YOUR SERVICE". Commissioned to celebrate HM The Queen's Golden Jubilee.

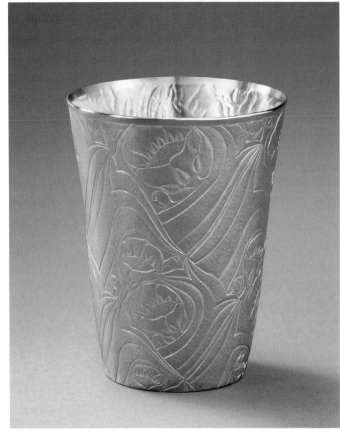

BEAKER, 2006

Britannia silver. Hand-raised and chased with gilt interior.
Purchase
Marks: Michael Lloyd, Edinburgh
Height 10cm · diameter 7.1cm

Slant sided form, chased in low relief with Scottish thistles as a circular motif.

Purchased following its inclusion at John Higgins' exhibition, as part of the 'Festival of Silver' held at The Goldsmiths' Centre, 2012.

BEAKER, 2012

Britannia silver. Hand-raised and hand-chased.
Buttercup motif. Matt finish, gilt interior.
Purchase
Marks: Michael Lloyd, Edinburgh
Height 10cm · diameter 8cm

BEAKER, 2013

Britannia silver. Hand-raised tapered form, hand-chased. Matt finish, gilt interior.
Gift of Mr Richard Agutter.
Marks: Michael Lloyd, Edinburgh
Height 10.5cm · diameter 8.4cm

Commissioned as one of a pair of water beakers by Mr Richard Agutter, Prime Warden of the Goldsmiths' Company 2013–2014, for use by the Prime Warden and his or her partner at Court and Livery Dinners at Goldsmiths' Hall. The chased theme is of the national emblems of the United Kingdom; the rose for England, the daffodil for Wales; the thistle for Scotland and the shamrock for Northern Ireland in the form of a circular pattern around the beaker.

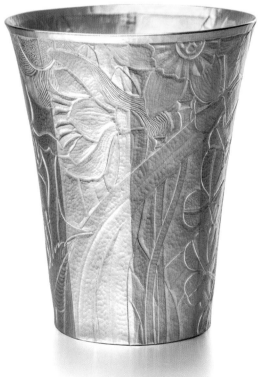

Detail

Drawings from sketchbook

BOWL, 2009

Britannia silver. Hand-raised and hand-chased bowl inlaid with fine gold, on forged stand. Gilt interior.
Commission
Marks: Michael Lloyd, Edinburgh
Bowl: height 14.5cm · diameter 25.8cm
Stand: height 7cm · width 20cm

Commissioned to commemorate the year of office of Mr Martin Drury, a former Director-General of the National Trust, as Prime Warden of the Goldsmiths' Company 2005–2006. This bowl's design and imagery which evokes nature grew from a quote by Octavia Hill, one of the founders of the National Trust: 'THE NEED OF QUIET, THE NEED OF AIR, THE NEED OF EXERCISE, THE SIGHT OF THE SKY AND OF THINGS GROWING, SEEM HUMAN NEEDS COMMON TO ALL MEN'.

ESTHER LORD

'My work is inspired by the spatial interaction between objects, structures and patterns in the natural and human landscape. I am fascinated by the effects of light and shadow on natural and man-made surfaces.

I collect initial design material from a wide range of sources, sketching and taking photographs all the time to build a visual library, studying images, objects, landscapes and places which contain inspiration, or even just give a feeling; an aesthetic which resonates.

I am inspired by silver. It is a very beautiful and highly responsive material, and I want to express this in my work. An important aspect is the play of light on silver. Folds combined with textured surfaces really emphasise its reflective qualities, and its ability to interact with its surrounding environment. It has the ability to totally change its character, and colour, depending on how it is lit, and where it is placed in a room.

I feel that there is something very instinctive about making vessels. They are an archaic or primal form, and there is a universal preoccupation in art, sculpture and rituals with vessels, and with containment as a tool for the communication of abstract ideas and meanings. This means vessels have a resonance beyond just being a functional item and I hope that they work as sculptural pieces as well.'

Born 1981. Master's degree, Birmingham City University, 2006.

Esther Lord constructs her work from a single sheet of silver, using scoring and folding techniques to shape the vessel as well as raising over a wooden former. The folded seams are then soldered. She ends with a hand-emery finish to give a soft satin sheen texture. Her studio workshop is in Birmingham.

Public Collections include:
2008 'Etched Wedge and Fused Layer' Vessels, The Museum of Modern Art and Design, Munich, Germany.

Drawings

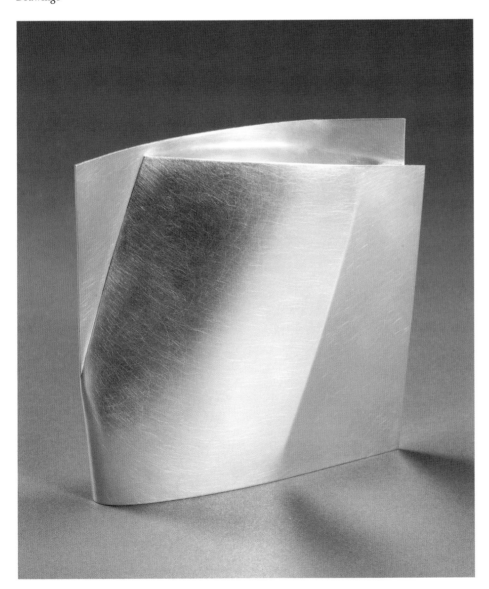

'DIAGONAL OVERLAP' VASE, 2009

---

*Hand-scored, folded and textured. Made
from one continuous sheet of silver.
Purchase
Marks: Esther Lord, Birmingham
Height 13.3cm · width 14cm*

The vase with its subtle texture and
sculptural form explores the effects
of light and shadow and the contrast
between soft curves and angular folds.

'TILTING' VESSEL, 2010

*Britannia silver. Constructed from a single
sheet of silver. Scored and folded angled body
with two diagonal folds on one side and four
diagonal folds on the opposite side. Raised
over a wooden former to create the soft
curves to contrast with the crisp folded seams.
Matt finish.*
Commission
Marks: Esther Lord, Birmingham
Height 31cm · width 27cm

'Tilting' Vessel is inspired by the action
of lifting and pouring. The aim was to
capture movement in this piece; the
form transfigured, folding in upon itself
or drawing upwards, away from the
horizontal surface.

  The concern is with balance and the
tipping point, the moment of stillness
before a transformation, and the effect
of the diagonal in juxtaposition with
the horizontal, which creates dynamism
and a feeling of movement.

WATER JUG, 2010

Formed from a single sheet, hand-scored, free hand-folded using handmade tools, then raised over a wooden former. Matt emery paper finish.
Purchase
Marks: Esther Lord, Birmingham
Height 32.5cm · width 11cm

Intended to be an elegant sculptural form as well as a functional object. The tapered jug's finish creates a subtle linear texture, designed to catch the light as it falls on the angular surfaces, accentuating the luminosity of the silver.

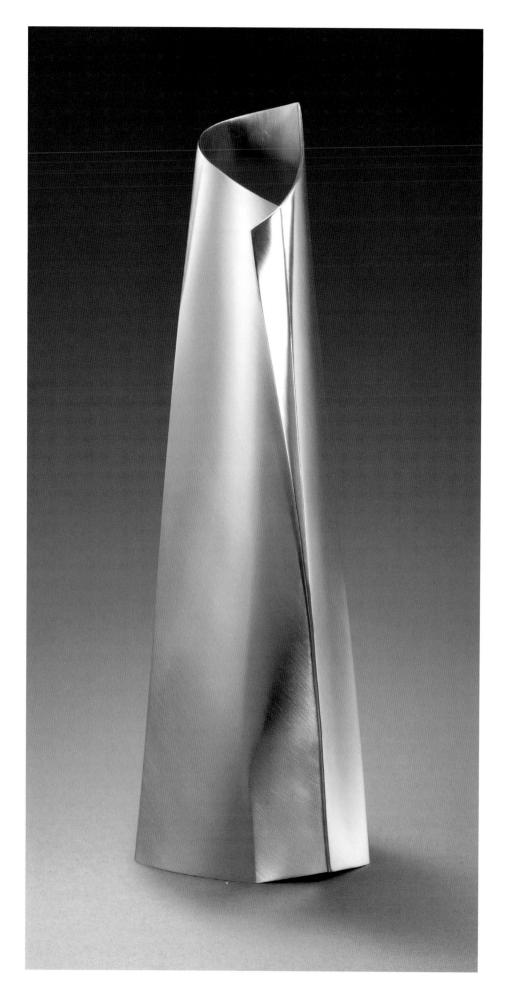

ANNA LORENZ

as a tool for crossing the boundaries from the material to the immaterial.'

Born 1967 in Germany. Graduate University of Central England, School of Jewellery, Birmingham, 2003. Master's degree of Fine Art, Birmingham. Tutor, The Institute of Art and Design, Birmingham City University.

Anna Lorenz uses the traditional techniques of raising and piercing but in new directions. Her studio workshop is in Birmingham.

Public Collections include:
2003 Wire Ball, Grassi Museum, Leipzig, Germany.

Selected Commissions include:
2003 Trophy, IAFF World Championship in Athletics, Birmingham City Council;
2004–6 Young Directors of the Year award, Trophies for the Institute of Directors, Birmingham;
2010 Set of Brooches, Jewellery Quarter Museum's Commission, Birmingham.

'The overriding themes of my work are structure, space, depth and transparency, often coupled with interaction or an element of surprise.

    Apart from seeking inspiration in my everyday surroundings, I research into contemporary architecture and art. I am particularly interested in the work of the Japanese architect Tadao Ando whose buildings emphasise empty space to represent the beauty of simplicity in relation to Zen Philosophy.

    Also, Juhani Pallasmaa claims that: 'the ultimate meaning of any building is beyond architecture; it directs our consciousness back to the world and towards our sense of self and being. Significant architecture makes us experience ourselves as complete embodied and spiritual beings. In fact this is the great function of all meaningful art'.

    I have been to Tadao Ando's 'the Church of Light' and 'the Water Temple' in Japan and experienced the enveloping calmness of the spaces. I aim to translate this experience into work that allows for layers of interpretation and personal associations. I use the process of cutting and repetition

Drawings

BOWL, 2009

Britannia silver. Stamped squares out of a silver blank. Raised using a horn mallet. Scratch brush finish with hand-burnished highlights.
Purchase
Marks: Anna Lorenz, Birmingham
Height 14cm · diameter 23.5cm

The raising of the bowl distorts the geometric shapes to create a final form which plays with light and shadow enhanced by the sparkle of the burnished edges. The fruit bowl was purchased from Goldsmiths' Fair, 2009.

'EMBRACE' BOWL, 2011

Pierced silver and copper discs using a square stamping tool to create a mesh grid. Then raised using a horn mallet. Scratch brush finish to the silver bowl. Oxidised finish to the copper bowl on Welsh slate plinth.
Purchase
Marks: Anna Lorenz, Birmingham
Silver bowl: height 12cm · diameter 19.5cm
Copper bowl: height 11.8cm · diameter 20cm
Slate base: length 30cm · height 2cm · width 10cm

The two half spheres can sit separately or fit inside each other introducing an element of playfulness, interaction and variation of use as bowls. The consideration of strong visual impact, both by harmony and contrast, is explored in this piece. 'Embrace' Bowl was purchased from Goldsmiths' Fair, 2011.

OLIVIA LOWE

'I specialise in designing and making sculptural silver vases. My inspiration comes from the flowers themselves, and through my work I create new forms where the vase itself is as interesting as the flowers it holds. My work explores the relationship between natural objects such as flowers, and the contrasting qualities of silver, bringing them together to create a single composition where both elements are of equal visual importance.

Designing and working in metal enables me to express my awareness of objects in their environment and the interest I have towards the visual interpretation of objects by people. I enjoy the challenge of finding a new way for silver to fulfil a conventional purpose.'

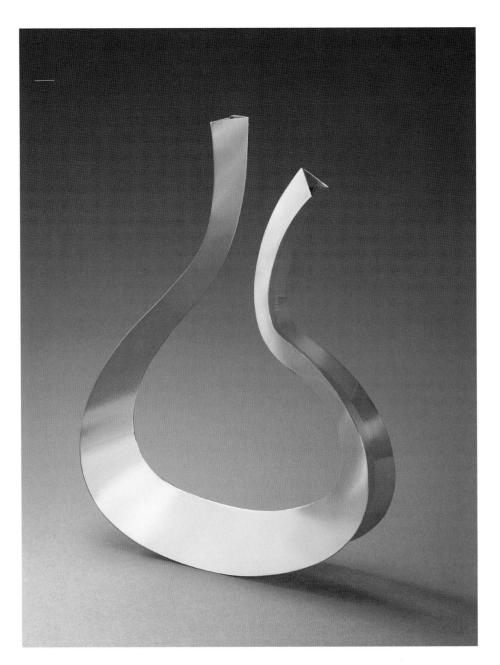

Born 1981. Master's degree, Royal College of Art, 2006.

When making sculptural silver vessels, Olivia individually hand-forges long strips of silver into two-dimensional curves, before bending them up into three dimensions and fitting and soldering them together to create the three-dimensional linear vessel. Her studio workshop is in Hampshire.

Selected Commissions include:
2006 'Just the Two of Us' Vase, Royal College of Art Collection, London;
2008 'Slavery I' Medal, Swedish Royal Coin Cabinet, Stockholm, Sweden;
2011 'Silver Chalice', The Church of the Blessed Mary, Upham, Hampshire.

'VESSEL' VASE, 2013

Formed using four long strips of silver, each hand-forged to produce four flat, curved pieces. These are then bent up into three dimensions, fitted and soldered together to create the three-dimensional linear vessel.
Commission
Marks: Olivia Lowe, London
Height 24cm · width 17.8cm

The crisp edges of the vase emphasise the graceful fluidity of its linear form. Rather than this vase merely performing the physical function of containment, the resulting arrangement is one in which the silver and flowers combine to form a unified sculptural object.

FRANCES LOYEN

Selected Commissions include:
1985 Rosewater Bowl, The Worshipful Company of Mercers;
1986 Badge and Chain, Sheriff of the City of London;
1989 Four Water Jugs, St John's College, Cambridge;
1998 Tabernacle, Elmore Abbey, Berkshire.

The Goldsmiths' Company Modern Silver Collection (not included in the exhibition):
1981 Goblet;
1983 Two Bowls.

THREE 'WHISKY TOT' BEAKERS, 2004–2005

Spun beakers with plique-à-jour enamel, two with gilded interiors.
Purchase
Marks: Frances Loyen, London
A: height 6.5cm · diameter 5.8cm
B: height 6.5cm · diameter 6cm
C: height 6.5cm · diameter 5.9cm

This work by Frances Loyen was first shown in the 'Silver on Sale' exhibition which accompanied the Company's travelling exhibition 'Treasures of Today' in 2005 at Millennium Gallery, Museums Sheffield.

'My designs are influenced by extended time spent in the study of plants and animals whilst working on the restoration of an ancient building in rural France as well as my urban life, in London.

The technique of plique-à-jour enamelling is used in my work only in the larger, three dimensional pieces: candlesticks, beakers and goblets. The size and form of each piece allows more scope for reflection of the colour around and inside the object and space- the colour is half seen, more subtle and mysterious.'

Born 1951. Graduate of Sir John Cass School of Art, 1975. Trained at Wright & Davies, Cartier's goldsmith workshop. An artist enameller who specialises in plique-à-jour enamel on silver. Frances has studio workshops in London and in France.

GRANT MACDONALD

'I have a number of criteria that steer me through my work; I have always enjoyed designing and making good, if not, great pieces of silver. Handmade means many things to different people; to me it means scarcity as well as exclusivity and quality. In my designs I try to bring together a fusion of traditional craftsmanship and new technology perhaps proving that the craft is always moving forward. True inspiration comes from knowing that by the extraordinary skills of the silversmith's craft almost anything is achievable. After more than forty years of designing it is also tempting to say that "to leave something tangible behind" is a potent thought.'

Born 1947. Graduate of Sir John Cass School of Art, 1969.

Grant Macdonald is a designer craftsman with a large London design workshop, employing 12 craftsmen, specialising in custom-made pieces of silver and gold for clients in the Arabian Gulf and in commissioned pieces for the City of London market and private collectors, using both traditional techniques and the latest technology such as rapid prototyping. He was the first silversmith to be awarded the Queen's Award for Enterprise in International Trade 2006. Annually around 90% of the pieces designed and created in house by Grant Macdonald are sold overseas. He was Prime Warden of the Goldsmiths' Company 2008–2009.

Selected Commissions include:
1977 Processional Cross, Southwark Cathedral, London;
1992 Gallery Tray, The Silver Trust for No.10 Downing Street, London;
1998 Orb & Cross, Frauenkirche, Dresden, Germany;
2002 Pair of Loving Cups, The Worshipful Company of Leathersellers, London;
2002 Freedom Casket gift to HM Queen Margrethe of Denmark from The Goldsmiths' Company;
2005 Lectern, The Worshipful Company of Actuaries, London;
2008 City of London Freedom Casket presented to President Sarkozy of France by the Lord Mayor on behalf of The Corporation of London.

The Goldsmiths' Company Modern Silver Collection (not included in the exhibition):
1975 Decanter;
1976 Two Paper Knives;
1977 Rose Bowl;
1981 Asprey Two-Light Candelabra;
1983 Sword;
2000 Paper Knife;
2002 Travelling Photograph Frame.

PAIR OF TWO-LIGHT CANDELABRA, 2011

Opposing 'C' form. The two sides of each arm of the piece were fabricated by making a curved steel tool and hammering the two halves of silver sheet over it, an inner and an outer piece.
Commission
Marks: Grant Macdonald, London
Height 36cm · width 48cm

Commissioned to mark the year of office of Mr Grant Macdonald as Prime Warden 2008–2009. A challenging design to make in silver in that it involved hammering sheets of silver into opposite curves at the same time.

The design symbolised the Company's agreement to start the building of the Goldsmiths' Centre as Grant Macdonald was Prime Warden at the time of this momentous decision.

The relevance to this historic moment is in the measurements of the candelabra; they are seventeen and a half inches wide overall to represent the seventeen and a half million pounds spent on the project, and they are five inches wide across the base to represent the five floors of the new building at the Centre. The candelabra are now used and lit on the table at Livery Dinners at Goldsmiths' Hall.

GRANT McCAIG

'Silver carries with it a significant history. As silversmiths we work with this history as we do the metal. I work exclusively with fine silver for my "Pleated" range. The forms themselves tend to be fairly simple, echoing familiar domestic objects, often contrasting silver with found or recycled wood. The "Pleated" tumblers have evolved from a fascination with a simple process of folding the metal repeatedly which creates both visual rhythm and structure to finished works.'

Born 1974.Graduated from Glasgow School of Art 1998, BA Hons, Design and Applied Arts, Jewellery and Silversmithing. Master's degree, Royal College of Art, 2011. Lecturer, Department of Silversmithing and Jewellery, University for the Creative Arts, 2013 – present day.

Grant McCaig uses traditional skills of fabrication and forging often combining other materials with silver. Grant's work often celebrates the forms shaped for sea travel, or the way in which the sea shapes or colours all things involved with it. He is inspired by nature or nature's effect on manmade objects. His studio workshop is in London.

Public Collections include:
2000 Finger Bowl, Birmingham Museum and Art Gallery;
2008 Two Serving Spoons, National Museums Scotland, Edinburgh;
2012 Chelsea Tea Strainer, Aberdeen Art Gallery, Scotland.

Selected Commissions include:
1998 Trophy, Scottish Engineering Company of the Year Award;
1999 Chain of Office, for Lord Provost, Edinburgh;
2000 Fruit Bowl, the Incorporation of Goldsmiths, Edinburgh, loaned to Bute House, Edinburgh;
2006 Silver Whisky Set, 10/10 Silver Collection, the Incorporation of Goldsmiths, Edinburgh;
2007 Mace, Queen Margaret University, Scotland.

'HARBOUR' SUGAR AND CREAM SET, 2007

Fabricated and seamed vessels, gilt interiors with forged silver spoon on a reclaimed oak wood serving tray with a silver rim.
Purchase
Marks: Grant McCaig, Edinburgh
Tray: height 2cm · diameter 17.8cm
Sugar Bowl: height 5.4cm · length 14.7cm width 6.2cm
Spoon: length 13.3cm · width 2cm
Cream Jug: height 11.6cm · width 6.5cm

Inspired from vessels shaped for sea travel, the sugar bowl is boat shaped and has a curved bottom whilst the cream jug resembles the prow of a ship. These combined with the wooden tray gives the set its nautical connection.

CARAFE AND TWO BEAKERS, 2009

Seamed, folded and hand-raised. The repeated folding and unfolding of the silver creates a ridged pattern before final folding, seaming and hand-raising.
Purchase
Marks: Grant McCaig, Edinburgh
Carafe: height 18.5cm · diameter 6.5cm
Beaker 1: height 6.6cm · diameter 6.3cm
Beaker 2: height 6.9cm · diameter 6.3cm

Taking inspiration from Japanese textiles, this work is about the use of texture and surface decoration. Here the linear quality of the pleated metal creates a characteristic visual rhythm and structural strength overall.

ALISTAIR McCALLUM

'I have always had an interest in colour and contrast and this has always played a central role in my work. I have expressed this through materials and how these can be manipulated to achieve different results. This interest led me in 1976 to the Japanese metalworking technique of Mokume Gane. At the time there were few practitioners and very little technical or visual reference material, so through a process of trial and error I developed my own interpretation of the technique. I wished to innovate rather than emulate traditional Japanese work. Though the technique works well on a jewellery scale I felt it would benefit from an increase in scale where there is a larger surface area to explore the relationship of pattern to form. This led me to becoming a silversmith rather than a jeweller. I strongly believe that the technique is only part of the design process and that the relationship of function pattern and form needs to be understood and work together to achieve a successful piece.'

Born 1953. Master's degree, Royal College of Art, 1978. An artist craftsman practising the traditional Japanese metalworking technique Mokume Gane. Literally translated Mokume Gane means 'wood grain' metal and involves sandwiching together layers of different coloured metals, rolling them into a sheet, then creating a pattern by breaking the surface layer to expose the metals beneath. Alistair's studio workshop is in London.

Public Collections include:
1979 Pill Box and Bowl, The Crafts Council, London;
1984 Dish, Birmingham Museum and Art Gallery;
1987 Box, Leeds City Art Gallery;
1987 Box, The Crafts Council, London;
1988 Bowl, National Museums Scotland, Edinburgh;
1989 Two Bowls, Leeds City Art Gallery;
1991 Bowl, Art Gallery of Western Australia;
1992 Server, The Rabinovitch Collection at the Victoria and Albert Museum, London;
1995 Bowl, Shipley Art Gallery, Gateshead;
1999 Bowl, Brighton Museum and Art Gallery;
1999 Three Beakers, Brighton Museum and Art Gallery;
2000 Vase, Birmingham Museum and Art Gallery;
2003 Bowls, Birmingham Museum and Art Gallery;
2003 Two Bowls, Manchester Art Gallery;
2005 Lidded Bowl, Birmingham Museum and Art Gallery;
2010 Bowl, Museum für Kunst und Gewerbe, Hamburg, Germany;
2010 Dish, Ashmolean Museum, Oxford.

Selected Commissions include:
1997 Ladle, Millennium Canteen, Millenium Gallery, Museums Sheffield;
1998 King George VI and Queen Elizabeth Diamond Stakes Trophy, De Beers, London.

The Goldsmiths' Company Modern Silver Collection (not included in the exhibition):
1980 Mokume Gane bowl;
1983 Two Mokume Gane bowls;
1996 Mokume Gane bowl.

VASE, *c.*2002

Silver, copper and gilding metal. Mokume Gane on the outside surface, matt finished silver on interior surface. Made from six layers of silver copper and gilding metal individually silver soldered together. The laminate is then rolled to produce a sheet.
Purchase
Marks: Unmarked
Height 20.5cm · diameter 7.8cm

The pattern on this vase was achieved by breaking through layers to produce the pattern but also to create a subtly faceted surface. A landmark piece and the beginning of a new direction in Alistair McCallum's work.

MOKUME GANE DISH, *c.2007*

Circular patterned dish formed with four layers
of silver and gilding metal.
Purchase
Marks: unmarked
Height 6cm · diameter 22.3cm

This piece was purchased from
Goldsmiths' Fair, 2007.

TWO BEAKERS, 2014

Spun with Mokume Gane rim made from 12 layers of silver copper and gilding metal which has been made into a square bar then twisted into a spiral before being forged back into a square bar.
Purchase
Marks: Alistair McCallum, London
Height 8.8cm · diameter 7.4cm

The beakers were purchased from Goldsmiths' Fair, 2014, as examples of domestic ware.

SHEILA McDONALD

*South House Workshop,
Shetland*

*'I like to work from my coloured source
drawings and sketches developing one idea
into a whole range of design possibilities.'*

Born 1958. Graduate of the Glasgow
School of Art, 1980. Master's degree,
Royal College of Art, 1984. Guest Fellow
Bishopsland Educational Trust.

Sheila originally studied Textile Design
at the Glasgow School of Art and these
strong elements of textile and drawing
inspire her current design work. In her
enamel pieces, she combines several
traditional enamel techniques in a
painterly way, working with colours;
bold and bright, or subtle with fine
layers of transparent colours over gold
and silver foil. Sheila shares studio
workshops with her husband Rod
Kelly, silversmith, both in Norfolk
and Shetland.

Shetland cliffs

*Drawings and enamel
test pieces*

Detail, 'Shetland Bird' vase, 2013

View from South House.
2012

Watercolours and drawings

'SHETLAND BIRD' VASE, 2013

Hand-raised vase, decorated with gold and silver foil and enamel, etched and engraved silver.
Commission
Marks: Sheila McDonald, London
Height 14cm · diameter 15cm

The design for this vase was inspired by Sheila's drawings of the landscape in Shetland; the rugged formations of the sheer cliffs and the wheeling, circling birds. The intention was to capture a strong feeling of movement, both in the sweep of the asymmetrical shape of the vase and the design of the birds in flight around the cliffs.

The main body of the vase was etched to suggest cliff faces. A monotone palette of grey, black and transparent enamels, building up the enamels in layers, adding areas of 24ct gold and fine silver foil with each firing, was used to convey the sense of atmosphere of these remote islands at the top of Britain, 120 miles north of the Scottish mainland.

This was Sheila's first large scale commission allowing her different creative disciplines of draughtsmanship, painting, textile design and jewellery design to be expressed in a larger scale. It has led her now to create a new series of silver beakers each painted in enamel with natural images, featuring wildlife observed in Shetland and Norfolk.

ANGUS McFADYEN

Born 1962. Graduate of Manchester Polytechnic, 1984. Tutor Wrexham College of Art 1984–1988.

Angus McFadyen is an artist engraver; he hand-raises his forms which he then carves and engraves with his designed decoration, which begin as detailed drawings. His studio workshop is in Derbyshire.

Public Collections include:
1996 Cake Slice, The Rabinovitch Collection at the Victoria and Albert Museum, London.

Selected Commissions include:
2000 Tea Set, The Pearson Collection;
2013 Clock, The Pearson Collection.

'I find inspiration quite a difficult subject to get straight in my mind. I can think of lots of things that influence what I make and how I make it but "inspire" is a very big word. Things that I respond to and which influence me include pattern, drawing, fossils, textiles, fabric, form. Of course the work of other metalworkers would also be an influence. I can't deny that Japanese metalwork, new and old, is something to which I am always drawn. The interest lies not only in the finished objects but also some of the techniques and the skill with which they are used.

In fact, now I think of it, it is perhaps the work of other makers that I do find inspirational. The more I have learned about how things are made, and the more time I have spent trying to make things well, the more I respect and admire the skill needed to make the very best work. So I suppose if I were to choose one thing that inspires me it would be craftsmanship.'

Drawing

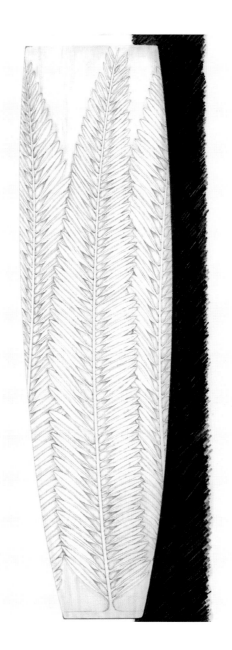

VASE, 2009

*Fine silver. Hand–raised vase engraved
and carved with images of fern leaves.
Pumiced finish.
Commission
Marks: Angus McFadyen, Edinburgh
Height 28.1cm · diameter 10.3cm*

Structured fern leaves are deliberately
designed to overlap and bind
together to make an overall pattern
defining the form of the vase.

VASE, 2013

*Hand-raised and then engraved with a
combination of a low relief honeysuckle and a
much flatter background pattern which reflects
the light differently according to the angle from
which it is viewed. This effect is achieved by
cutting slightly elongated dots at right angles to
each other.*
Marks: Angus McFadyen, Edinburgh
Height 12.5cm · diameter 8.5cm

The honeysuckle motif came from
a wallpaper pattern by Lewis F. Day
which Angus had been asked to
incorporate on a commission for a
university mace. The idea for the
background came from damascene
fabrics and wallpapers.

This vase was purchased from
Goldsmiths' Fair, 2013.

VASE, 2015

Hand-raised with inlay, hand engraved and carved with fine silver inlay.
Commission
Marks: Angus McFadyen, Edinburgh
Height 30cm · width 20cm

The decoration is in the form of leaves based on a climbing plant that Angus saw whilst on holiday. The vase was commissioned for a new display in 2015 of contemporary designed pieces by modern silversmiths. This display will be used on formal occasions in the Livery Hall of Goldsmiths' Hall as the Buffet Plate to highlight to the guests dining there the Company's role as a major patron of modern silver and the exceptional quality of the silver work.

WAYNE MEETEN

'One of the most important lessons I have learnt in becoming a silversmith is that everything you make comes from the heart.'

Born 1961. Graduate of the Sir John Cass School of Art, 1999, and Tokyo University of Fine Arts and Music, Japan, 1998, where he studied the techniques of Mokume Gane, Kinkeshi and Shibori.

His designs are based on his other passion, the Tai Chi Chaun and Chi Kung and Taoist philosophy.

Using the traditional Japanese techniques of Shibori and Japanese hammer chasing, he strives to give the metal a warmth and softness not only from the fluidic lines but the curvaceous forms he has chosen. His workshop studio is in Devon.

Public Collections include:
1999 Mokume Gane and Glass surround Bowl, Bristol Museum.

Selected Commissions include:
2000 Mokume Gane and Glass surround Bowl, Contemporary Arts Society, London;
2002 Mokume Gane Incense Burner, Rothschild Foundation, Exbury House, Hampshire;
2003 Water Jug, Rothschild Foundation, Exbury House, Hampshire;
2004 Mokume Gane Vessel, and Silver Platter Dish, Rothschild Foundation, Exbury House, Hampshire;
2005 'Fruition' Vessel, The Duke of Devonshire, Chatsworth House;
2011 Caddy Spoon, The Pearson Silver Collection;
2013 'Sunset' Finger Bowl, New College, Oxford;
2014 Fruit Bowl, British Allied Trades Federation and British Jewellers Association, Birmingham.

'STILLNESS IN FLIGHT' VASE, 2015

Hand-raised from single flat sheet, and Japanese hammer-chased.
Commission
Marks: Wayne Meeten, London
Height 35cm · width 18cm

The vase was commissioned for a new display in 2015 of contemporary designed pieces by modern silversmiths. This display will be used on formal occasions in the Livery Hall of Goldsmiths' Hall as the Buffet Plate to highlight to the guests dining there the Company's role as a major patron of modern silver and the exceptional quality of the silver work.

HECTOR MILLER

'Since childhood I have been making things in wood, stone and metal, so becoming a silversmith has been an excellent way to have used my practical skills and inventive talent. It has also brought me into contact with other wonderfully creative silversmiths and jewellers. I have been privileged as a member of the Goldsmiths' Company to help support many younger artists and craftsmen in a profession that has provided me with a lifetime of fulfilment.'

Born 1945. Master's degree, Royal College of Art, 1971. Consultant silversmith to the Goldsmiths' Company's Modern Collection Committee 1997–2004. Prime Warden of the Goldsmiths' Company, 2011–2012.

Designer silversmith who worked with Stuart Devlin, silversmith, but then established his own successful silversmithing company. His design workshop in London is equipped with both traditional tools and modern machinery such as a Tungsten Inert Gas (TIG) welder.

Public Collections include:
1995 Cake Slice, The Rabinovitch Collection at the Victoria and Albert Museum, London;
2002 Pair of 'Grebe' Candlesticks, the Victoria and Albert Museum, London.

Selected Commissions include:
1974 Dinner Service, The Shah of Persia;
1981 Trophies for the first London Marathon;
1990 Hanging Pyx, Portsmouth Cathedral;
1990 Pair of Coasters, The Worshipful Company of Pewterers, London;
1996 Pair of Waiters and Pair of Salvers, The Silver Trust for No.10 Downing Street, London;
2004 Ascot Diamond Stakes Rosebowl;
2006 'The Prince Albert Challenge Cup', Henley Royal Regatta.

The Goldsmiths' Company Modern Silver Collection (not included in the exhibition):
1975 Caddy Spoon;
1976 Water Jug;
1981 Pair of two-light Candelabra;
1986 Prototype Cutlery Set;
1991 Cigar Box;

1993 Three Mustard Pots and two Pepper Grinders;
1999 Freedom Ceremony Pen Stand;
2003 Four Courtroom Table Lamps;
2011 Trays.

TWO JUGS, 2014
(ONE ILLUSTRATED)

Made using a series of components that were hammered, formed or cast, the individual pieces fused into an integrated whole using mostly the TIG welding process. The internal liner made from thin stainless steel to reduce weight and a hinged lid integrated to hold back the ice when water is being poured.
Commission
Marks: Hector Miller, London
Height 33cm · width 18cm

The idea for these jugs, two of a set of three, came from the need to make iced water containers that would not drip condensation onto the leather surface of the Court Room table during Goldsmiths' Company meetings. In order to achieve this, Hector Miller designed a double skinned jug with the main body needing to be straightforward in shape to contain the liner, but the lip with its integrated handle and hinged cover had scope for creating a sculptural form which he worked out in a series of models.

Commissioned to commemorate the years of office as Prime Warden of the Goldsmiths' Company of Sir Jerry Wiggin, 2006–2007 and Professor Richard Himsworth, 2007–2008. Pair of a set to be used at meetings of the Goldsmiths' Company governing body, known as the Court of Assistants, held in the Court Room around an imposing table designed in the 1830s by the architect of Goldsmiths' Hall, Philip Hardwick.

JUNKO MORI

'My work is based on uncontrollable beauty through the growing process in the natural world. I like "odd" stuff amongst other perfect forms. In the eighteenth century natural historians were trying to discover the underlying laws governing nature and found that mutations can become a catalyst for new questions. I too continue my search for odd beauty in the natural world to create in metal from constituent parts a nucleus of a growing form.'

Born in Yokohama, Japan in 1974. Graduate of the Musashino Art University, Tokyo 1997. Junko then moved to the UK in 1997. Graduate of Camberwell College of Art, 2000.

Hand-forging is commonly used to make cutlery but Junko employs this technique to make multiple pieces, using hammers to create innovative silver forms. No piece is individually planned but becomes fully formed within the making and thinking process. Junko is inspired by nature's creations and is driven by the culture of her birthplace and Shinto beliefs where everything has life. Her studio workshop is in North Wales.

Public Collections include:
2001 Propagation Project, Leaf and Silver Organism, Square Spike, Crafts Council Collection, London;
2002 Silver Organism, Square Spike, Aberdeen Art Gallery, Scotland;
2002 Steel Organism, National Museums Liverpool, Merseyside;
2004 Silver Organism / Textured Spike, Birmingham Museum and Art Gallery;
2006 Silver Organism / Pine Cone and Steel Organism, Manchester Art Gallery;
2006 Silver Organism / New Pine, The Ulster Museum, Belfast;
2006 Silver Organism / Pinecone, National Museums Scotland, Edinburgh.

Selected Commissions include:
2001 Silver Organism, Square Spike, Sheffield Assay Office Collection;
2004 'Sprig', Foyer Sculpture, Peter Jones, London;
2008 'White Rose', Wall Sculpture, Residency and exhibition project organised by Yorkshire Art Space, Sheffield and Sheffield Assay Office.

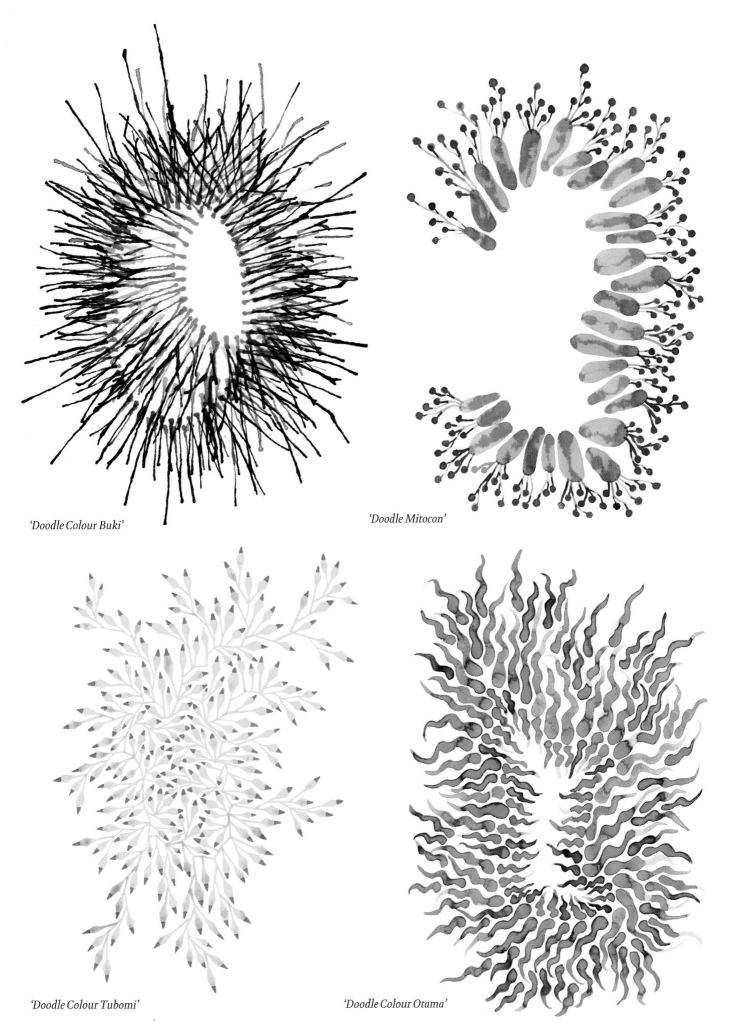

'Doodle Colour Buki'

'Doodle Mitocon'

'Doodle Colour Tubomi'

'Doodle Colour Otama'

'ORGANISM', 2005

Hand-forged multiple pieces, welded into one.
Purchase
Marks: Junko Mori, Sheffield
Height 14cm · width 14.5cm

This table sculpture can also be used as
a container.

'PINE CONE', 2007

Hand-forged fine silver TIG welded, flanges part-polished.
Purchase
Marks: Junko Mori, Sheffield
Height 16cm · width 17cm

The quality of fine silver allows malleability, ductility and high reflectivity. This piece resulted from a residency awarded to Junko Mori by the Harley Foundation, allowing unique access to a library of natural history collections amassed by Lady Margaret Cavendish, Duchess of Portland (1715-1785) and her descendants.

Junko Mori was drawn to Philip von Sielbold's *Flora Japonica 1835* illustrated with hand coloured line engravings precisely detailing botanical structure of plants and trees from Japan, unknown in the West at the time.

This piece was purchased through the contemporary decorative art dealer Adrian Sassoon, London, 2007.

Detail

THERESA NGUYEN

'As an artist silversmith, I simply love the creative process of designing and making an object for the first time. My desire is that a finished piece should feel like a beautifully composed piece of music, able to be spiritually uplifting, emotionally stirring, inspiring and beautiful.

I feel motivated by a sense of wonder about the world around me and my hope is that I will be able to draw from the incredible magic of creation and be able to somehow capture a little of its essence in my work, conveying a sense of organic form, and by incorporating sensuous surfaces, creative movement and flow.

Learning new and innovative approaches to working with silver has been invaluable to my on-going development as an artist silversmith.'

Born 1985 of Vietnamese origin. Graduate of the School of Jewellery, Birmingham City University 2007. Winner of the Goldsmiths' Company's 'Young Designer Silversmith Award', 2005.

Senior Fellow Bishopsland Educational Trust 2007-08. Artist in Residence for the Goldsmiths' Company's 'Studio Silver Today' exhibition series at Kedleston, Derbyshire, 2011, in liaison with the National Trust.

Theresa Nguyen specialises in the traditional skills of soldering, folding and forming techniques. Her studio workshop is in Birmingham.

Public Collections include:
2005 Cocktail Shaker and Drinking Vessels, Birmingham Museum and Art Gallery;

2010 'Con Brio' Centrepiece, The National Museum Wales, Cardiff.

Selected Commissions include:
2006 'The Robert Copeland Trophy', Tittensor Village Produce Guild;
2007 Sculptural Vase for Lord Coe, Birmingham City Council;
2007 Pair of Candleholders, Mr Robert Copeland;
2013 'Kairos' Centrepiece, The Worshipful Company of Clothworkers, London.

PAIR OF 'TAPERED ALCOVE' CANDLEHOLDERS, 2008

Britannia silver, fabricated using techniques of hand-scoring, folding and soldering. Polished by Elliot-Fitzpatrick Ltd to a 'Butler' finish.
Purchase
Marks: Theresa Nguyen, London
Large candlestick: height 25.2cm · width 16.5cm
Small candlestick: height 21.5cm · width 14.2cm
Detachable vase insert: length 17cm · width 2.8cm

Shaped as a twist, these candleholders capture the transition between two-dimensional and three-dimensional space. Soft sweeping curves, inspired by those found in the Bath terraces, are mirrored in both candleholders creating light-reflecting surfaces.

This design, second prize winner in the Company's 2007 'Young Designer Silversmith Award' was used by Theresa Nguyen to make up the pieces for 'Collect' 2008 at the Victoria and Albert Museum. These pieces subsequently won the NADFAS Achievement Award prize for best newcomer, as well as a Silver Award in the Silversmiths (Junior) section, a Gold Award in the Smallworkers (Junior) section and a Special Council Award in the Goldsmiths' Craft and Design competition, 2008.

'SWIRL' VASE, 2009

Britannia silver. Seamed and fabricated from one sheet of silver, then hand-raised, with hammered surface.
Purchase
Marks: Theresa Nguyen, London
Height 29cm · width 10.3cm

Exploring the concept of energy in a form, this vessel is constructed with four transitional twists. The dynamic sense of movement is further emphasised by the tactile textured detailing of the surface.

This vase was purchased as a result of the Bishopsland Educational Trust exhibition at The Victoria and Albert Museum, London, 2009.

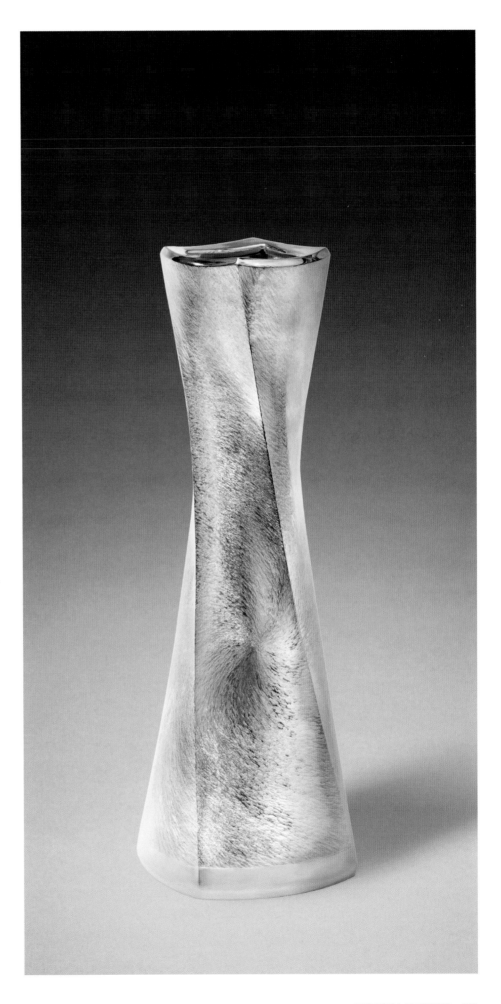

'PARISSA' CENTREPIECE, 2009

Two tiered centrepiece composed of individual leaf shapes soldered together to form small dishes. Bright whitened finish with highlighted edges.
Made with fold forming and hammering techniques. Formed over wood with nylon hammers with soldering carried out in stages.
Purchase
Marks: Theresa Nguyen, London
Top tier: height 6.5cm · width 14cm
Bottom tier: height 6.7cm · width 23cm
When assembled: height 8.5cm · width 21cm

Conceived as a conceptual and visual piece influenced by the botanical structure of the ripened leaves of a camellia japonica. The aim is to capture a fluidity and softness in silver to reflect a sense of growth. Purchased following its display in the Goldsmiths' Craft and Design Awards Exhibition, 2010.

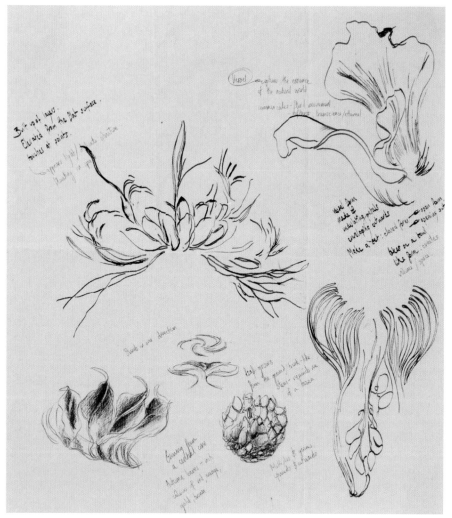

Sketchbook drawings

'SPIRITUS' CENTREPIECE, 2010

Britannia silver. Leaf shaped forms in swirling spiral pattern. Fold-formed, hammered, and soldered.
Purchase
Marks: Theresa Nguyen, London
Height 19.5cm · width 26.5cm · diameter 24cm

This design for an open and fluid form is inspired by the energy of natural growth and nature's response to the sun. The design refers to multiple leaves unfurling from a tightly packed centre. The flowing softness of the blades of leaves evokes the feeling of being energised and enlivened by the warmth of the sun.

Purchased following its inclusion in the Goldsmiths' Company's 'Mindful' exhibition, 2011.

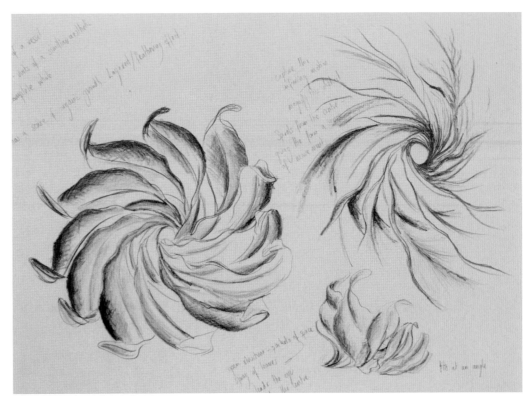

Drawing

CÓILÍN O'DUBHGHAILL

'The work here is part of a series investigating the colour possibilities of silver and gold alloys. For me this process and materials led research is central to silversmithing and the ongoing search for new possibilities and directions.

The driving forces of my work as a silversmith change over time and from project to project. It could be materials, process or content driven, asking questions, exploring things that perk my interest. What connects all the projects and keeps me going is the absorption of making, the therapy of time spent at the bench.'

Born 1974, Ireland. Graduated from Edinburgh College of Art, 1996. In 1998, he moved to Tokyo, to study in the metalwork department at the National University of Fine Arts and Music (Tokyo Geidai), receiving a doctorate in 2005. Visiting lecturer Glasgow School of Art, 2005–2007, Senior Research Fellow, Sheffield Hallam University, 2007.

Cóilín's work focuses on the exploration of vessel forms through a study of process, materials and colour, using a range of techniques and materials he acquired in Japan such as irogane (coloured metal alloys). He has developed new ways to construct and create patterns in metal and explore colour through patination and surface treatment. Cóilín's studio workshop is in Sheffield.

Public Collections include:
2003 'Tsukinjizou' (commuter shrine), public art, Toride City Collection, Japan;
2005 'Double Vision & Focus', Vessels, Irish State Art Collection;
2008 'Closed Segment' Vessel, National Museum of Ireland, Dublin;
2009 'Shakudo 2' Bowl and 'Shibuichi 3' Bowl, Crafts Council of Ireland, Department of Foreign Affairs;
2012 'Shibuichi 5', Bowl, Crafts Council of Ireland, Department of Foreign Affairs;
2013 'Ritual 9', Vessel, Irish State Art Collection.

Selected Commissions include:
1996 'Silvermouse', Computer Mouse, Birmingham Assay Office Collection;
2006 'Fairweather Communion Cup', Glasgow Cathedral;
2006 'Shibuichi 1', Bowl, Marzee Collection, Netherlands;
2007 'Tricycle' Teapot and Sugar Bowl, Incorporation of Goldsmiths, Edinburgh;
2010 'Crucible', Vessel, Galeria Sztuki w Legnicy, Poland;
2012 'Shakuko 4', Bowl, Marzee Collection, Netherlands.

SHAKUDO BOWL, c. 2011

A gold alloy was cast in a bar form using a continuous casting machine. The Shakudo alloy is 2% gold, 98% copper. The bar was rolled into thick sheet and hammer formed into the bowl shape using sinking, raising and planishing hammer techniques. The surface of the bowl was then selectively polished to remove some of the surface layer. The bowl was then patinated, dried and coated with renaissance wax.
Purchase
Marks: Unmarked
Height 10.5cm · diameter 22.2cm

Shakudo produces a dark patina resembling lacquer. It was historically used in Japan to decorate Katana fittings such as tsuba, menuki and kozuka. Here this revival of a 500 year old Japanese traditional technique produces a striking contemporary design. This bowl was the result from extensive research undertaken at Sheffield Hallam University into Shaduko by Cóilín.

SHIBUICHI BOWL, *c*.2011

Cast in a bar form using a continuous casting machine. The shibuichi alloy is 50% silver, 50% copper. The bar was rolled into thick sheet and hammer formed into the bowl shape. Sinking, raising, and planishing hammer techniques. The surface of the bowls were then selectively polished to remove some of the surface layer. The bowl was patinated, dried and coated in renaissance wax.
Purchase
Marks: Unmarked
Height 8.2cm · diameter 22.6cm

The two bowls in the Goldsmiths' Company Collection are developed from Cóilín's research into Japanese patination techniques. The Western tradition of metal patination and colouring is based on the use of a small range of metals and alloys that are coloured by the application of a wide range of patination solutions. In contrast to this, Japanese metalworkers developed a wide range of irogane (coloured metal) alloys that are coloured with a single patination solution. This approach has stimulated the development of a variety of methods to produce multi-coloured metalwork.

SHANNON O'NEILL

'I chose to study Three-dimensional Design at Manchester Metropolitan University. Working initially with ceramics and wood, my plunge into the world of silver began with a design for a water jug, which won the Goldsmiths' Company's 'Young Designer Silversmith of the Year Award'. Part of the prize was to help assist in the fabrication of the jug for two weeks, at the workshops of Nayler Brothers, under the tutelage of Tony Bedford. From there, I was hooked. Silver is such a wonderful medium to work with. It does require more persuasion than ceramics, but the goal is always to make it look effortless. My designs have always echoed the natural world around me. I'm looking for that moment of quiet; that moment where everything stops.'

Born 1971. Originally trained as a Ballet dancer. Graduate of Manchester Metropolitan University, 1995. Winner of the Goldsmiths' Company's 'Young Designer Silversmith Award', 1995. Artist silversmith in residence for the Goldsmiths' Company's 'Studio Silver Today' exhibition series at Dunham Massey, Cheshire, 2010, in liaison with the National Trust.

The curves and stance of Shannon O'Neill's silver work echo her background as a dancer and ceramicist, giving a sense of movement to her domestic pieces where there is always a point of balance. She mainly uses the traditional silversmithing techniques of hand-raising and hand-chasing to realise her hand-drawn designs inspired by the sea, music and dance. She is also a designer, restorer and model maker. Shannon's studio workshop is in Lincolnshire.

Public Collections include:
1995 Water Jug,
Manchester Art Gallery;
1998 Fish Slice, The Rabinovitch Collection at the Victoria and Albert Museum, London.

Selected Commissions include:
2002 Golf Trophy, Sir Peter Michael for the Pelican Centre on behalf of the Macmillan Trust;
2000 'The Lyndell Urwick Memorial Cup', The Institute of Directors as a gift to NADFAS chairman Australia;
2001 Millennium Salt Condiments, The Worshipful Company of Paviors, London;
2002 Pair of Candelabra, The Worshipful Company of Weavers, London.

The Goldsmiths' Company Modern Silver Collection (not included in the exhibition):
1999 Water Jug

'FIN' VASE, 2010

Fine silver and parcel gilt modelled in clay before remoulding and casting in wax. The wax model was electroformed. The piece was then filed, cleaned and polished to a 'Butler' finish.
Commission
Marks: Shannon O'Neill, London
Height 56.3cm · width 23cm

The vase design is of a fish's tail as it enters the water.

'DUNHAM MASSEY' BEAKER, 2011

Hand-raised and hand-chased. Bright finish.
Purchase
Marks: Shannon O'Neill, London
Height 11.5cm · diameter 9cm

The beaker is a copy of the demonstration one made at the National Trust property, Dunham Massey, in 2010 by Shannon O'Neill whilst Artist in Residence during the Goldsmith Company's 'Studio Silver Today' exhibition which featured her work. The original beaker was won by a member of the public during a prize draw at the end of the exhibition. The beaker oak frieze was inspired by the leaves of the stately oaks in Dunham Massey Park.

This exhibition series ran for five years (in 2010 at Dunham Massey, in 2011 at Kedleston, 2012 at Ickworth, 2013 at Erdigg and 2014 at Belton) in liaison with the National Trust. Five women artist silversmiths demonstrated their creativity and silversmithing skills during the period the houses were open to the public. Each silversmith involved in this exhibition series made a silver beaker inspired by the house or landscape of the National Trust property. This then formed part of the exhibition allowing the public to engage with the skills of silversmithing. Overall, 500,000 visitors to these exhibitions witnessed contemporary silver in Britain for the very first time.

Drawing

STEVEN OTTEWILL

'Whilst at The North Secondary School in Ashford, Kent, I was inspired to be become a silversmith by my metalwork teacher Mr Kay. I studied from the age of 13 and this was to be my chosen profession to my family's dismay at not carrying on the family tradition of cabinet making.

Ottewill Silversmiths and Jewellers Ltd now trades with clients globally and employs 22 people designing and building pieces of gold objets d'art, silverware and jewellery.

This year the company has invested heavily in new technologies and aims to grow the CAD and 3D RP side of the business as well as five axis machining.

My inspiration has always been the work of Jensen, with its fluid tapering lines realised wonderfully when translated into silver.'

Born 1968. Graduate of Kent Institute of Art and Design, 1990.

Stephen's design and studio manufacturing workshop is in rural Kent employing specialist craftsmen to make tableware, corporate giftware and commemorative items.

Public Collections include:
1993 Fish Slice, The Rabinovitch Collection at the Victoria and Albert Museum, London.

Selected Commissions include:
1993 Rose Bowl, Candlesticks and Water Jug, Lucy Cavendish College, Cambridge;
1994 Chalice and Paten, Canterbury Cathedral;
1996 Silver and Lapis Fish Server, University of Washington;
1996 Ceremonial Mace, Glasgow Caledonian University;
2000 Font Bowl and Ewer, Southwark Cathedral;
2007 Ceremonial Mace for the University of Cumbria;
2007 Processional Verger's Wand for St Albans Cathedral;
2007 Silver Wyvern, HMS Drake;
2009 Prince of Wales Cup, Henley Royal Regatta;
2009 Pineapple Cups and Goblets, Henley Royal Regatta;
2010 BBC Antiques Master Trophy;
2010 Championship, League One and Two Football Trophies for 'nPower';
2012 Mace, Birmingham University;
2012 Working with Barber Osgerby on the development and manufacturing the prototypes of the Olympic Torches for London 2012;
2013 Commemorative Bowl, Middlesex University.

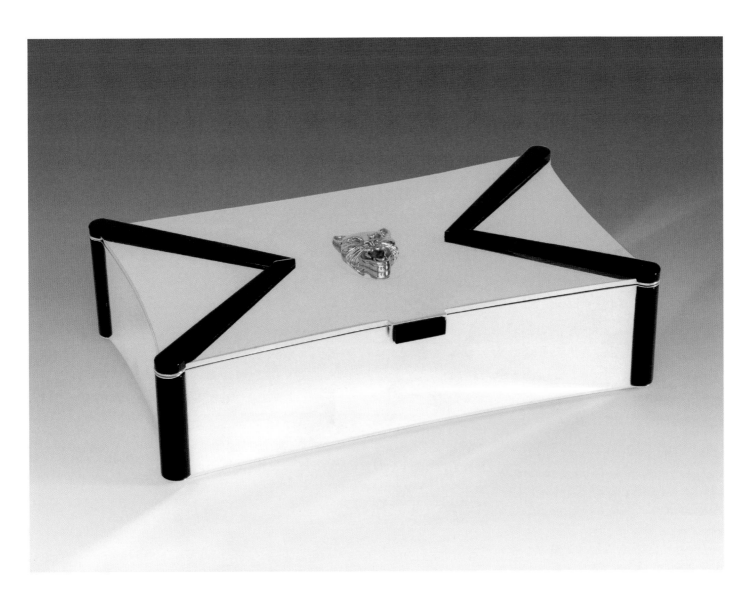

CIGAR BOX, 2004

*Hammered sheet fabricated into shape, fitted
with black obsidian strips and set with silver-
gilt leopard's head, carved by Mary Dean.
Commission
Marks: Steven Ottewill, London
Height 6.5cm · diameter 26.8cm*

This cigar box was commissioned
for domestic use at Livery Dinners
in Goldsmiths' Hall. The custom of
smoking cigars after dinner has now
ceased.

CARL PADGHAM & ANDREW PUTLAND

The partnership of these two silversmiths is called Padgham and Putland.

Using traditional silversmithing techniques, as designer silversmiths they mainly produce modern domestic silver and sporting trophies for the trade and retailers, in particular bespoke pieces for Bulgari. They also specialise in producing silver model buildings, vehicles, yachts, aircraft and animals. Their design workshop is in Kent.

CARL PADGHAM

'Having been brought up in an environment of hand craft skills, from cabinet making, model making, engineering and fine art and being surrounded by such tools, I was bound to start to dabble with these. With my family always working in these crafts looking to produce items of art, I could see how anything was possible, and that I could always realise whatever I could design.

Designing outside the box and thinking I could improve any object, and then craft with any material to a high standard was the goal.

Silversmithing is a way I found to achieve this aim, precious metals are such a good medium to work with and bring a real value to the time spent crafting a new piece.'

Born 1963. Graduate of Medway College of Design, 1984. Carl Padgham is the design force behind the team whose work is characterised by heavy gauge pieces with clean, modern lines.

ANDREW PUTLAND

'I've been interested in silversmithing since the age of fourteen. I amalgamated metalwork, art and technical drawing to find the perfect outcome.

I love the whole process from designing, manufacturing by manipulating and forming the metal, to finishing the piece and seeing the delight on the client's face.

I get inspiration from many aspects of life including nature, people, and my experiences.'

Born 1963. Graduate of Medway College of Design, 1984.

Selected Commissions include:
1990 Pair of Loving Cups, The Worshipful Company of Butchers, London;
1991 Flagon, Lichfield Cathedral;
2003 Thirty-one pieces of ecclesiastical silver commissioned by Bulgari for Dio Padre Misericordioso Church, Rome;
2007 Loving Cup, commissioned by John Papworth for The Worshipful Company of Clothworkers, London;
2009 Ceremonial Mace, Imperial College, London;
2012 Pair of Large Ballroom Chandeliers, Bulgari Hotel, Knightsbridge, London.

The Goldsmiths' Company Modern Silver Collection (not included in the exhibition):
1985 Sugar Bowl and Spoon, Milk Jug, Tray, Tea Pot;
1991 Water Jug;
1994 Salt and Spoon.

Church Dio Padre Misericordioso, Rome, 2003 by Richard Meier, architect.

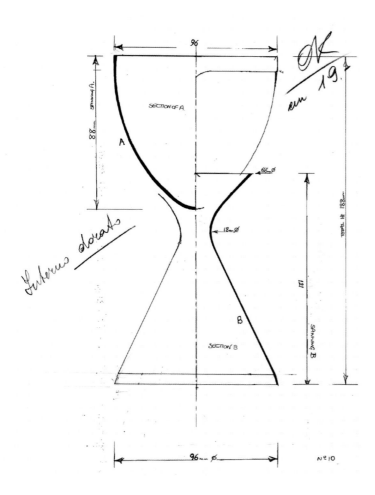

Design drawing

CHALICE, 2014

Britannia silver. Fabricated and hand-raised.
Commission
Marks: Padgham and Putland, London
Height 19.5cm · width 10cm

The Parish Church Dio Padre Misericordioso, 2003, was designed by the renowned American architect Richard Meier for the Churches in Rome project 2000. Nicola Bulgari, an ardent admirer of contemporary silver, commissioned 31 items of ecclesiastical silver from Padgham and Putland for the church as a donation from Bulgari. The recurring use of the octagon shape throughout the pieces is reminiscent of ecclesiastical gothic forms giving the silver an air of monumentality in keeping with the majestic sweeping modern lines in the concrete and glass of the building. The silver was used for the first time in a dedication ceremony on 26th October 2003 presided over by the Pope's representative, Cardinal Camillo Ruini.

This chalice was commissioned to commemorate this act of silver patronage as well as mark Nicola Bulgari's personal support of several British contemporary silversmiths following his first visit in 1990 to see the Goldsmiths' Company's Modern Silver Collection, conducted by the Company's Curator.

CHRISTOPHER PERRY

'I think I was always destined to work with silver, with my father having his own silver manufacturing and restoration business. However, I found education to be enlightening in terms of what could be designed and produced with silver. Until entering further education I had not dreamed that I could develop and make ideas using silver, and this really interested me.

I aim to challenge convention in design by using my traditional skills and asking 'what if' as I work through the techniques and processes to make a finished piece.'

Born 1974. Graduate of Sheffield Hallam University, 1997. The Goldsmiths' Company's Silversmithing Award presented at New Designers in 1997. Master's degree 3D Metalwork, Jewellery & Related Products BIAD School of Jewellery, Birmingham, 2001. Associate Lecturer, Sheffield Hallam University, 2003–present day.

After graduating, Christopher Perry joined Brian Asquith, silversmith, sculptor and industrial designer.

He later worked in the workshops of Howard Fenn and Richard Fox, before establishing his own workshop using the traditional techniques of silversmithing to create his designs. Christopher's studio workshop is in Sheffield.

Public Collections include:
2005 Fish Slice, The Rabinovitch Collection at the Victoria and Albert Museum, London;

'SQUEEZED' VASE, 2015

Scored and folded curves
Commission
Marks: Christopher Perry, Sheffield
Height 20.3cm · width 13.5cm · depth 11cm

The form was developed from the letter K. Christopher Perry wanted the curves to be enhanced and to push the metal further than normal, so came up with the idea of making a press tool to emboss the metal before scoring and folding. The result was an interesting new process.

This piece was commissioned following a similar vase being shown at the Goldsmiths' Fair, 2014.

2007 Orb Salt and Pepper Grinders, Museums Sheffield.

Selected Commissions include:
2003 Cleaver, The Worshipful Company of Butchers, London;
2006 Presentation Dish, Thoresby Estate, Nottinghamshire;
2008 St Leger Stakes Trophy;
2012 Goblet, The Worshipful Company of Cooks, London.

DON PORRITT

'My aim is to create significant sculptural form out of a ductile metal and by so doing produce unique functional silver, which has a distinctive and strong dynamic line.

Designs must express a strong sense of growth, movement and vitality – a reaching for dynamic imagery in silver. Essentially, the designer is working in a sculptural manner, shaping and manipulating the ductile metal to create forms in space.

This creative process requires an insight into the quality of light and how this can reveal and define the planes, contours and textures of the finished piece.

The exhilaration of taking a raw initial concept and shaping it into a significant and unique artefact is the essence of the designer's motivational experience.'

Born 1933. Graduate of the Leeds College of Art, 1963. Don's studio workshop is in West Yorkshire.

Inspired by the fluidity of water, Don Porritt's approach to creating vessels is essentially sculptural, the manipulation of form, plane and texture balanced by a

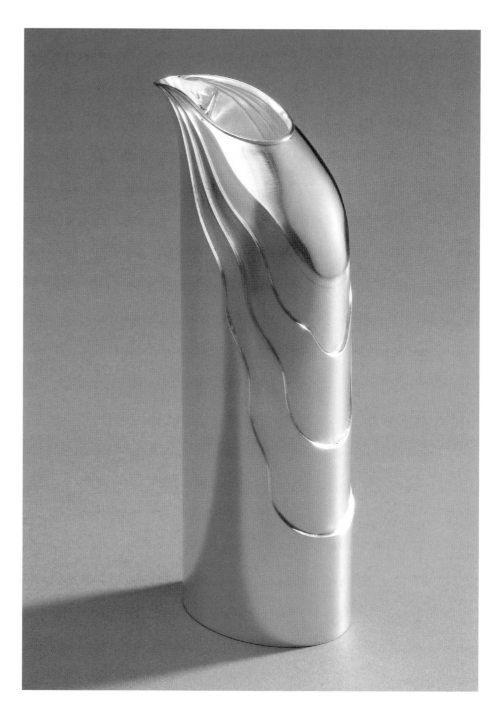

regard for practical, functional silver.

Don uses the traditional silversmithing skills, particularly hand-raising, casting, fabrication, forging, piercing and etching, all of which are selectively employed to bring the design concept into reality.

Selected Commissions include:
1977–78 Pair of Altar Flagons, Ripon Cathedral.

FLAGON, 2004

Part hand-raised and fabricated with a flowing curvilinear formation. The sharply modelled lines and planes are created as a result of an overlap technique which is used to build up the body, section by section.
Purchase
Marks: Don Porritt, Sheffield
Height 19.7cm · width 9cm

The relatively slim oval body fits neatly into the hand so no handle is required. The flagon is a variant on a theme Don Porritt has developed, giving attention to differential surface detailing or texture.

ALEX RAMSAY

'Being commissioned to make a bespoke piece is a journey, a chance to take the essence of something, be it a personality, a place, an organisation or an occasion, and capture it in the form of a unique object.'

Born 1973. City & Guilds Silversmithing, Hand Silversmithing & Jewellery, 2002. Assistant in Howard Fenn and Alfred Pain workshops, 2002.

Alex's studio workshop is in London where she uses traditional silversmithing skills of hand-raising and hand-piercing in particular. Her designs are often inspired by the ethereal powerful shapes and colours found in nature, a fascination that arose during time spent amongst the mountains and lochs of western Scotland and Iceland. Intriguing surface textures, pattern and depth emerge through the layering of materials.

Selected Commissions include:
2000 Millennium Centrepiece, the Worshipful Company of Engineers, London;
2008 Bowl, Beijing Olympics, gift to the Mayor of Haiden Province.

'POSITIVE AND NEGATIVE' PAIR OF BOWLS, 2009

Silver Bowl
Fine silver. Hand-raised, hand-pierced sheet, double skinned bowl.
Commission
Marks: Alex Ramsay, London
Height 10cm · diameter 15cm
Glass Bowl
Hand blown glass made in Hungary with copper oxide to give random patterning in the glass.
Fitted silver rim
Height 10cm · diameter 15cm

These bowls, inspired by silver nitrate photography, explore ideas of positive and negative, light and dark, reflection and shadow. The patterns in silver explore and reference those in the glass so that the two objects become a unique pair, balancing and reflecting one another.

CLARE RANSOM

'An intuitive approach to the making process expresses my fascination with details of the natural world through line, form and surface texture as I explore the intrinsic qualities of silver as a craft material. Using hammers and punches worked over nylon formers I manipulate a single sheet of silver, drawing it inwards into soft, flowing organic bowls and vessels. There is a spiritual element to my work, celebrating the season's growth and renewal.'

Born 1964. Graduated with a BA (3D Design Metalwork & Jewellery), Surrey Institute of Art and Design, 2005, MA (Contemporary Craft Practice), University of the Creative Arts (formerly Surrey Institute of Art and Design), 2007. In 2005 Clare won the New Designers Goldsmiths' Graduate Award for silversmithing and in 2006, she won two gold awards at the Goldsmiths Craft and Design Council Awards. Senior Fellow Bishopsland Trust. A second career silversmith, Clare's studio workshop is in Surrey.

Public Collections include:
2007 Bowl, The P&O Makower Trust loaned to the Ashmolean Museum, Oxford for their permanent collection.

Clare Ransom's workshop

'FOLDED' VESSEL BOWL, 2005

*Fine silver. Hand-raised, using adapted
hammers and punches over nylon formers
to stretch and fold the metal. The sheet of
silver is gathered and pleated into shapes. An
adaptation of the traditional 'crimping' method
of raising. Satin finish with burnished edge.
Purchase
Marks: Clare Ransom, London
Height 11.5cm · diameter 16.5cm*

Clare's inspiration is taken from
closely observed natural forms such
as windblown grasses, textured tree
bark and tide patterns in sand. Stylised
patterns are drawn directly on to the
silver, dictating the final form and
surface texture, which emerges through
the making process.

'Folded' Vessel Bowl was purchased
following Clare winning the New
Designers Award for silversmithing in
2005 with this piece.

ALEXANDRA RAPHAEL

'Plique-à-jour bowls! Blood, sweat and tears. Obsession with a degree of masochism are essential. Not for the faint of heart. I'm always pushing the envelope in uncharted territory and hence one of the most challenging of the art forms.

I have been fascinated by jewellery from early age and greatly inspired by my mother, an artist and gallery owner. Many of my designs are a reflection of my childhood memories. I have concentrated on the technique of enamel. There is no other medium that gives you such glorious colours. The bold reds, blues and golds to subtle pastel, glide between my ribbons of silver and gold cloisonné wire reflected by the precious metal below. What a wondrous medium with which to work! Over the years I have developed my own personal style and symbolism. I enjoy creating special pieces for individuals – tiny pictures in wire and glass – telling a story or inspiration. Power from the magic stones and beads incorporated in the jewel. A talisman depicting a history and secret message if the viewer examines closely.'

Born in the United States of America, 1945. Self-taught, Alexandra's studio workshop is in London where she specialises in cloisonné and plique-à-jour enamel using gold, silver and semi-precious stones.

Public Collections:
1984 'Moon Necklace', Musée Municipal de l'Evêché, Limoges, France;
1986 'Frog and Tadpole' Bowl, Musée de L'Horologerie, Geneva, Switzerland;
1988 Bowl, Musée Municipal de l'Evêché, Limoges, France;
1991 Bowl, Musée Municipal de l'Evêché, Limoges, France;
1991 Necklace, Museum for Decorative, Applied and Folk Art, Moscow, Russia;
1993 Bowl, Museum for Decorative, Applied and Folk Art, Moscow, Russia;
2013 Earrings, Musée Municipal de l'Eveche. Limoges, France.

BOWL, 2004

*Plique-à-jour enamel, 14ct yellow gold rim
and base with 24ct wire securing plique-
à-jour enamel.*
Commission
Marks: Alexandra Raphael, London
Height 8cm · diameter 13cm

Celestial imagery shows planet
movements, lunar changes, Zodiac
signs and a dancing leopard with
stars for spots symbolising the
Goldsmiths' Company.

PAMELA RAWNSLEY

'Although where I live in mid-Wales is not a place of 'pastoral idyll', it is capable of great beauty – always with an underlying threat, a sense of struggle for survival. Landscape in all its moods has always been important: the curve of a hill, a glimpse of light on rock, gushing water, big spaces containing tiny details. These are all first beginnings. My aim is for each piece I make to have a quiet presence, while its function and its meaning is suggested but not explicit.'

Born 1952. Died 2014. Studied Foundation Studies at Sir John Cass College, 1969–71, Jewellery at Herefordshire College of Art, 1979–80 before setting up her first workshop in 1981. Crafts Advisor, Arts Council of Wales, 1999–2003. Visiting Lecturer, University of Wolverhampton, 2001–4. Mentor, Bishopsland Educational Trust, 2010–11.

Pamela Rawnsley lived in Wales where her studio workshop looked out directly at the landscape which was so influential in her work. Her lyrical sequences of vessels evoke rhythms and patterns of light, line and atmosphere. The use of fabricated forms from silver sheet, fly-pressing to press-form sections which were then soldered and scoring and folding techniques were the dominant methods used by her to realise her concepts, which began with her drawings and prints before being translated into metal.
Pamela was inspired by many artists including the land artist Richard Long. She was admired by her contemporaries for her unique expressions in silver, her responses to her continuous preoccupation with landscape, and the ambiguity and shape-shifting nature of natural light.

Public Collections include:
1983 Inlaid Resin Jewellery, the Victoria and Albert Museum, London;
2000 Vessel, Shipley Art Gallery, Gateshead;
2006 Group of Vessels, Aberdeen Art Gallery;
2006 Group of Vessels, National Museum Wales, Cardiff;
2009 Silver Vessel Sequence, National Museums Northern Ireland;
2009 Silver Vessels, Contemporary Art Society of Wales, Cardiff and National Museum Wales, Cardiff (joint purchase).

Selected Commissions include:
2004 Vessel, The Guardian Hay-on-Wye Festival of Literature Madoc Award.

'SHADOW' VESSELS, SERIES, 2004–2005

Made from silver sheet formed in sections using a flypress, (four sections to each vessel), then cut assembled and finished with a 'Renaissance Wax' coating. Roller-printed and oxidised.
Purchase
Marks: Pamela Rawnsley, London
Small Shadow Vessel:
Height 22.4cm · width 5.5cm
Tall Shadow Vessel:
Height 32.7cm · width 7cm
Medium Shadow Vessel:
Height 28cm · width 6cm

Inspired by the Welsh mountains of her home, 'Shadow' vessels are tall, narrow and deliberately shallow forms, in silver. They are an interpretation of the ambiguity and shape-shifting nature of the landscape of mid-Wales. The constantly changing light transforms the mountains from solid masses to flattened silhouettes, and alternately reveals and obliterates detail. The vessels are designed as a group of related forms with two distinct profiles. Primarily to be viewed from the front, as the viewer moves past or around them the slim profile from the side allows them to almost disappear, while the matt finish contributes to an ethereal quality.

Purchased from The Harley Gallery, 2004, following her solo exhibition there.

'THREE DAYS' VESSEL SEQUENCE, 2007

*Fabricated from sheet, formed and soldered
with the linear attachments being press-formed
in two sections, then soldered. Matt finish with
gilded interiors of respectively black, lemon,
and hard yellow gold.*
Commission
Marks: Pamela Rawnsley, London
Vessel with black interior:
Height 14cm · width 7.3cm · length 19cm
Vessel with lemon interior:
Height 11.8cm · width 7.2cm · length 17cm
Vessel with hard gold interior:
Height 11.5cm · width 7.2cm · length 16cm

A related group of forms to express
both the passing of time and a sense of
timelessness. The artist was inspired
by the powerful sense of place and the
resulting strong connection one feels
when one returns to the same area but
sees it anew when viewed at different
times of day, month or year.

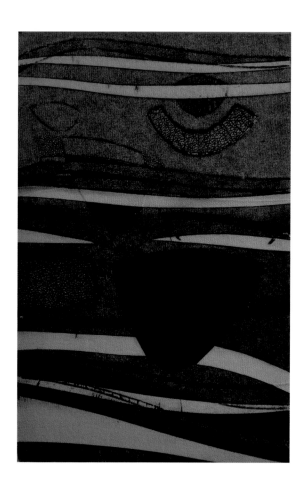

*Collagraph, 2006, relating to
'Three Days' Vessel sequence.*

'OUT OF THE BLUE' THREE BEAKERS, 2013

Three small cups, one part-gilded, one with oxidised detail, one just silver, all with matt finishes. Fabricated from thin sterling silver sheet, scored and folded, punched dotted lines on all three, with additional roll-printed lines on one.
Purchase
Marks: Pamela Rawnsley, Edinburgh
Height 7.5cm · diameter 6.5cm

The inspiration for these cups came from Pamela's visit to Australia in autumn 2012 as an invited artist in residence at 'JamFactory', Adelaide.

Part of the project was to experience extraordinary landscapes including desert, bush, and ancient volcanic ranges, all a complete contrast to the landscape at home in Wales which informed her earlier work. She was particularly struck by the fragility of the eco-system while out in the bush and the contrasting exotic quality of the flora, and above all the vastness of it all. Here her initial response, of which these cups are part, is to make small and intimate pieces which enable a fluid, direct and spontaneous way of working in deliberately thin material.

The 'Out of the Blue' Beakers were purchased through Ruthin Craft Centre, 2013.

Collagraph, 2013, the image relates to her 'Out of the Blue' series of beakers

FRED RICH

'The attraction to colour and bright sparkly things has been with me from my earliest memories, and the wonder and delight in the world around me seems to get more intense as I get older. Although I've been working professionally for nearly 35 years I still feel that I've fallen into this by accident and at some point I will have to start a proper job.'

Born Spain 1954. Graduate of the Central School of Art 1981. Winner of the Jacques Cartier Memorial Award, awarded by the Goldsmiths' Craft and Design Council in 1997, 2001 and 2003 for outstanding craftsmanship.

Fred's studio workshop is in Sussex where he specialises in colourful enamelling using the techniques of cloisonné, champlevé and basse-taille to portray representational images of natural flora and fauna. Designs originate in his vibrant water colours.

A versatile craftsman, he has skills in the distinctive fields of silver, jeweller and art medals, but above all he is considered a master enameller with respect to technique.

Public Collections include:
1998 Pair of Candlesticks, the Victoria and Albert Museum, London;
2007 Ink Stand, Keatley Trust, loaned to the Fitzwilliam Museum, Cambridge.

Selected Commissions include:
1988 Trophy, King George VI and Queen Elizabeth Diamond Stakes for De Beers;
1989 Primates Plaques, for Lambeth Palace Chapel;
1991 Choristers' Badges, Lichfield Cathedral;
2001 Millennium Vase, The Worshipful Company of Ironmongers, London.

The Goldsmiths' Company Modern Silver Collection (not included in the exhibition):
1982 Vase;
1996 Vase.

BEAKER, 2005 (ENAMEL 2009)

Spun body with burnished wires and 22ct gold rim. The body is textured and pickle finished with bright highlighted lines and cloisonné enamelled motifs.
Purchase
Marks: Fred Rich, London
Height 10.3cm · diameter 6cm

Leaping salmon is the starting point. The idea is kept fresh and simple by the sense of fast flowing water through bold graphic lines of rectangular wire, burnished to contrast against a carved, matt silver background. The richly encrusted form shows a new direction in the work of this artist enameller.

LINDA ROBERTSON

'My work relates to the urban environment in which I live. Having been born and lived on a small island off the West Coast of Scotland for 25 years, it was so refreshing and exciting for me when I moved to the city (Glasgow). It was this urban environment which was to first inspire my work, and which continues today to inspire me.

I travel through the city, often by foot. I take inspiration from the architectural landscape; even the common drain cover has featured in my work.

I feel that the architecture of the city is directly linked to the architecture of the table. I see buildings as functional containers, vessels holding objects and people, so I reflect this in bringing urban architecture to the table through my functional silverware. This landscape is made up of objects with different functions and forms, from the sauce bottle to vessels, creating this miniature table top skyline.

I work mainly in sheet metal, using restrained geometric forms.'

Born Isle of Bute, Scotland, 1965. Graduate of Glasgow School of Art, 1997. Master's degree, Royal College of Art, 2000. Tutor of Silversmithing at Central St Martins and at Richmond upon Thames College. Fellow Bishopsland Educational Trust 1997–98.

Linda Robertson uses spinning, press-forming as well as traditional silversmithing hand-skills. Her studio workshop is in London.

Selected Commissions include:
2000 Rosewater Bowl, the Worshipful Company of Weavers, London;
2000 Condiment Set, the Incorporation of Goldsmiths, Edinburgh and loaned to Bute House, Edinburgh;
2005 Tea Pot, 'Silver of the Stars', Incorporation of Goldsmiths, Edinburgh.

Below left: Linda Robertson's sketchbook showing inspiration from road markings

Below right: Taken from Linda Robertson's sketchbook; street drain, used as inspiration for 'Two Streams Vinaigrette'

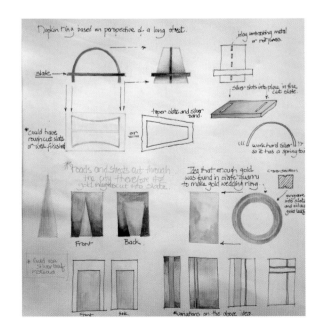

'TWO STREAMS' VINAIGRETTE, 2001

Seamed fabricated vessel, partially formed on stakes. Spout hand-scored and folded, shaped so the vinaigrette will pour in two streams. Bright finish.
Purchase
Marks: Linda Robertson, London
Height 24cm · width 7.3cm

The simplicity of the design gives elegance to this functional, domestic piece.

CARAFE, 2000

Scored, seamed and fabricated. Small plate soldered inside adjacent to lip to control flow. Gold inlay decoration on matt finished body.
Purchase
Marks: Linda Robertson, London
Height 26cm · width 7cm

Inspired by Glasgow city architecture.

CHALICE, 2004

*Spun with fine gold inlay, matt surface finish, knop with raised inscription
'THE BLOOD OF CHRIST'.
Commission
Marks: Linda Robertson, London
Height 28cm · width 14.2cm*

Linda Robertson's first commission for an ecclesiastical chalice which conveys the serene beauty of the geometry of form.

'VARIATION' TEAPOT, 2008

*Spun, fabricated, laser-cut, photo-etched with parcel gilding. Insulated teapot lid and insulating ring separating the outer body from the inner section which holds the tea.
Commission
Marks: Linda Robertson, London
Height 12cm · width 20.5cm*

A variation of the celebrity singer Lulu's chosen design for the 'Silver of the Stars' exhibition at the National Museums Scotland, Edinburgh, commissioned from Linda Robertson in 2005 by the Incorporation of Goldsmiths for the City of Edinburgh. The exhibition involved the pairing of ten international celebrities in the fields of film, music, theatre and literature with ten of Scotland's finest silversmiths. Each pair collaborated on the design brief silver for 'a drink with a close friend', resulting in a varied collection of drinking vessels from goblets to teapots to claret jugs.

The overall shape of this teapot is inspired from stacking pebbles seen in Feng Shui gardens. The minimal design is intended to convey spirituality, underpinning the ceremonial ritual of tea drinking.

MICHAEL ROWE

'For me it has always been important to question established approaches to creativity in studio metal and, through exploring its foundations and contexts, to evolve new strategies for originating form.'

Born 1948. Master's degree, the Royal College of Art, 1972. Awarded the Golden Ring of Honour from the German Association of Goldsmiths, 2002, an Honorary Doctorate from the University of Buckingham, 2004, and an Honorary Doctorate from the University of Hasselt, Limburg, Belgium, 2010, all awarded for services to Silversmithing. Fellow and Senior Tutor at the Royal College of Art 1984 – present. His work is notable for its innovative approach to form and concept. Michael Rowe's particular interest is the use of geometry in the expression of ideas and concepts relating to containers, vessels and other hollow-ware that are central to the silversmith's art. To express these concepts he uses fabrication and forming over steel stakes, with

hand-finishing. His studio workshop is in London.

It should be noted that 25 European and International museums and public institutions have 46 examples of Michael Rowe's work dating from 1973 to 2011.

Public Collections include:
1973 Double inkwell, Aberdeen Art Gallery and Museums, Scotland;
1978 Box, Victoria and Albert Museum, London;
1980 Bowl, Birmingham City Museum and Art Gallery;
1983 Cylindrical vessel, Badisches Landesmuseum, Karlsruhe;
1985 Cylindrical vessel, Art Gallery of Western Australia; Perth;
1988 Conical vessel, Pinakothek der Moderne, Munich;
1992 Conical vessel, Vestlandske Kunstindustrimuseum, Bergen;
1993 Cylindrical vessel, Stedelijk Museum, Amsterdam;
1993 Conical vessel, National Museum of Modern Art, Tokyo;
1994 Conical vessel, Museum Boymans van Beuningen, Rotterdam;
1994 Lidded container, National Museums Scotland, Edinburgh;
1994 Conical vessel, Museé des Arts Decoratifs, Paris;
1994 Conical vessel, Nordenfjeldske Kunstindustrimuseum, Trondheim;
1994 Conical vessel, Museum of Contemporary Applied Arts, Turin;
1997 Lidded container, 21st Century Museum of Contemporary Art, Kanazawa;
1999 Cubic vessel, National Gallery of Australia, Canberra;
2002 Fish server, the Victoria and Albert Museum, London;

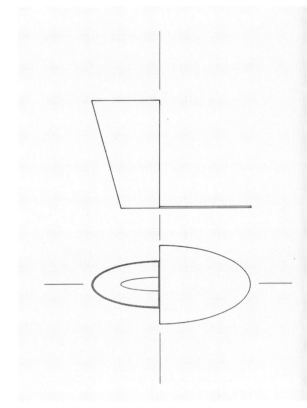

Design drawing for 'After Euclid' Jug, 2006

2002 Cup, the Millennium Galley, Museums Sheffield.

Selected Commissions include:
1980 Dish, West Midlands Arts, for Birmingham Museum and Art Gallery;
1994 Pair of Candelabra, the Silver Trust for No.10 Downing Street, London;
2002 Cup, Sheffield Assay Office, for the Millennium Commissions Project, Millennium Gallery, Museums Sheffield;
2010 Bowl, New College, Oxford.

The Goldsmiths' Company Modern Silver Collection (not included in the exhibition):
1999 CFO 31: Conical Vase.

'AFTER EUCLID' JUG, 2006

Constructed from sheet silver, formed over steel stakes and hand-finished.
Commission
Marks: Michael Rowe, London
Height 19.9cm · width 24cm

Here the jug form is formulated into a new geometrical structure but still retains a visual presence as a pouring vessel. 'After Euclid' is a series of quietly subversive silver pieces based on the geometry of ellipses. In the jug the traditional elements: body, spout, foot are playfully reconfigured into a new structure where the spout becomes the container, the foot defines a non-existent body, and in the absence of a handle the vessel is lifted by the spout, ambiguities that disturb expectations.

This jug was commissioned following Michael Rowe's retrospective exhibition at Birmingham Museum and Art Gallery in 2003.

TOBY RUSSELL

'The process of designing and making work enables me to take an idea through to completion and it is this attempt to perfect the visual and tactile qualities in three dimensional form that gives me most satisfaction as a silversmith.

The influences behind my designs are a combination of the plasticity of organic forms such as coastal formations, desert landscapes and the reflective qualities of water with an architectural awareness of modernism.'

Born 1963. Graduate of Camberwell College of Art, 1986.

Toby Russell specialises in scoring and folding sheet to create dynamic visual forms, inspired by the writings of Charles Jencks on architecture. His studio workshop is in London.

Public Collections include:
1990 Pewter Vase, the Victoria and Albert Museum, London;
1994 Cake Slice, The Rabinovitch Collection at the Victoria and Albert Museum, London;

Selected Commissions include:
1996 Fruit Stand, The Silver Trust for No.10 Downing Street, London;
2000 Ceremonial Mace, The London Institute;
2002 Alms Dish, York Minster;
2002 Rosewater Bowl and Loving Cup, The Worshipful Company of Haberdashers, London;
2006 Loving Cup, The Worshipful Company of Clothworkers, London.

The Goldsmiths' Company Modern Silver Collection (not included in the exhibition):
1992 Vase;
1994 Bon Bon Dish;
1995 Pair of candelabra;
1996 Napkin Ring.

'MILLENNIUM BOWL', 1999

Bowl consisting of 14 leaves created by scoring, folding and block forming. Polished by Reg Elliot of Elliot Fitzpatrick Ltd.
Millennium commission
Marks: Toby Russell, London
Height 20cm · diameter 44cm

Inspired by engineered matching structures and rhythmic patterns of natural forms. The concept here is to reflect a visual balance of opposing elements. The artist silversmith was conscious of the balance between technological sophistication and the preservation of the natural world being issues considered critical at the turn of the new century in 2000. This bowl was commissioned from Toby Russell when he was 36 years old by the Goldsmiths' Company to celebrate the Millennium.

One of the four major Millennium commissions, the bowl featured in the Company's exhibition 'Treasures of the Twentieth Century' where a third of the Company's Modern Collections represented the 20th century.

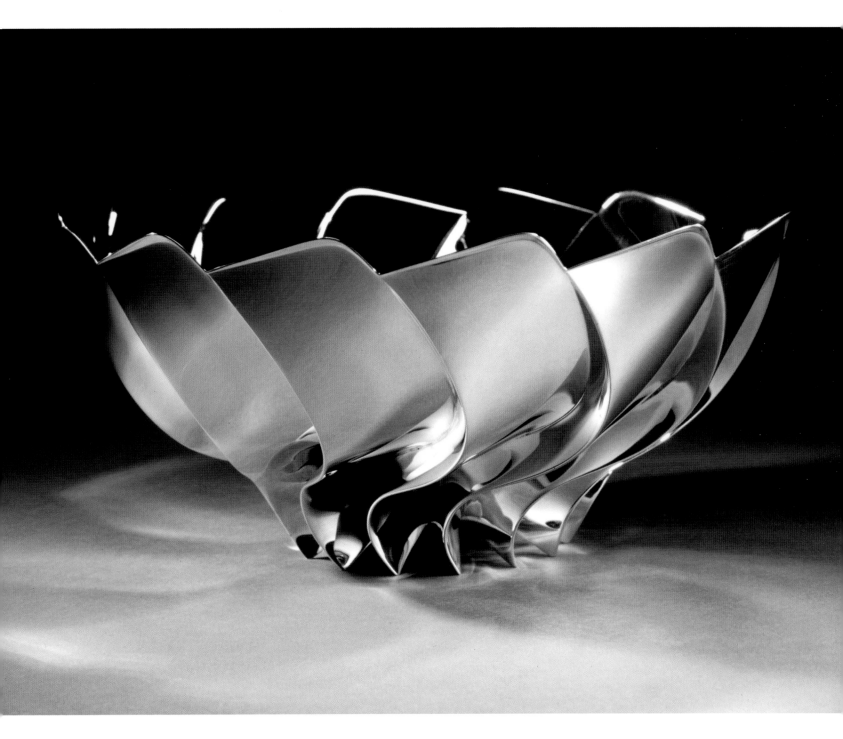

JANE SHORT

'I have been fascinated by the possibilities in the technique of enamelling since I was first introduced to enamels in 1974, whilst training to become a jeweller at Central School of Art and Design.

I see my work as a continual exploration into the possibilities within the technique of enamelling and indulging in the wonderful range of colours available to me. In some of the work I am interested in subtle harmonies of colour, reflecting observations from nature. At other times the richness and vibrancy of colours provoke a more personal imagery.

My work combines the techniques of engraving with enamelling in the form of champlevé and baisse-taille, where areas of metal are removed and filled in with enamel – the background of these areas being carved with detail which shows through the enamel. This produces a rich and painterly effect. Although in the past I have tended to cover as much of the surface as possible with enamel I am currently exploring the effects of contrasting areas of carved and engraved metal with areas of enamel. My current work is focusing on more geometric patterns, playing with contrast of shape and colour.'

Born 1954. Graduated Central School of St Martins, 1975. Master's degree, Royal College of Art, 1979. Tutor and Senior Fellow Bishopsland Educational Trust

Winner of the Jacques Cartier Memorial Award, awarded by the Goldsmiths' Craft and Design Council in 2008 for outstanding craftsmanship.

Jane Short combines the techniques of engraving and champlevé and basse-taille enamel to produce rich painterly images which begin as her watercolour designs followed by enamel test pieces. Her studio workshop is in Brighton.

Public Collections include:
1984 Enamelled Dish, Shipley Art Gallery;
1987 'Chameleon' Rocking Vase, National Museums Scotland, Edinburgh;
1992 Fish Server, The Rabinovitch Collection at the Victoria and Albert Museum;
1995 Vessel, Hove Museum and Art Gallery;
2002 Commemorative Dish, The Keatley Trust, Fitzwilliam Museum, Cambridge;
2007 Four Seasons Tazza (collaboration with Clive Burr), the Keatley Trust at the Victoria and Albert Museum, London;
2008 Landscape Vessel (Valerie's Vase), Ashmolean Museum, Oxford.

Selected Commissions include:
1991 Wafer Box, Lichfield Cathedral;
2001 Presentation Piece for Millennium Bridge, City of London opening, HM The Queen's Collection;
2002 Dish, The Worshipful Company of Weavers, London;
2003 Mantlepiece Clock (collaboration with Clive Burr), The Silver Trust for No.10 Downing Street, London;
2004 Font Plug, Welbeck Chapel, Welbeck;
2011 Centrepiece, The Worshipful Company of Clothworkers, London.

The Goldsmiths' Company Modern Silver Collection (not included in the exhibition):
1990 Vase.

'MILLENNIUM DISH', 1999

Engraved with champlevé and basse-taille enamel by Jane Short, spun bowl section by Clive Burr, silversmith.
Millennium Commission
Marks: Jane Short, London
Height 5cm · diameter 35cm

This dish was commissioned by the Goldsmiths' Company to celebrate the Millennium. The Millennium celebration itself is represented by enamel flames (bonfire) and fireworks (stars) around the centre of the dish. The rim, with its subtle engraving and pastel enamel highlights, suggests the tiny place of humanity within the vastness of the universe of all time, represented by wind, water and rock formations. This concept of all time is echoed in the central void, its empty space evocative of time future.

One of the four major Millennium commissions, the dish featured as an iconic statement in the Company's exhibition 'Treasures of the Twentieth Century' where a third (569 exhibits) of the Goldsmiths' Company's Contemporary Collections of silver, jewellery and art medals represented the 20th century.

'LICHEN' BEAKER, 2007

Spun beaker, carved and engraved with champlevé enamel, with gilded interior.
Commission
Marks: Jane Short, London
Height 9cm · diameter 6.7cm

The pattern on this beaker is an abstract representation of a lichen covered stone surface. The aim was to achieve a subtle evocation of the colours and textures observed in the natural world.

'FISH SCALE' BEAKER, 2006

Spun beaker, carved and engraved with champlevé enamel and decorative gold pallions, with gilded interior.
Commission
Marks: Jane Short, London
Height 9cm · diameter 6.8cm

The pattern is based on close observation of the colours and textures of fish scales, especially those of Bream and Bass, where there is no distinct patterning but a gradual change of colour.

'LEOPARD SKIN' BEAKER, 2006

Spun beaker, carved and engraved with champlevé enamel, gilded interior.
Commission
Marks: Jane Short, London
Height 7cm · diameter 6.9cm

Although the design is a reference to the heraldic leopard of the Company's coat of arms, the patterning of the engraved fur texture and coloured enamel echoes the patterning variance found on a real leopard where each spot is a little different to the next. One of four beakers commissioned to celebrate the natural environment.

'SNOWFLAKE' BEAKER, 2008

Spun beaker, carved and engraved with champlevé enamel.
Commission
Marks: Jane Short, London
Height 7cm · diameter 6.9cm

The pattern is based on the individual patterns of snowflakes, in this case

sectored plates, stellar plates and stellar dendrites. The focus on this basic molecular structure of the ice crystal is enhanced by the pale cool colours of the enamel and the overall tonal quality of the silver.

Jane says 'we often see representations of snowflakes on the paraphernalia of a modern Christmas, but these are usually only a crude approximation of the delicate and fascinating beauty of the actual snowflake. I was also intrigued by the way that the basic molecular structure of the ice crystal dictates the flake's six fold symmetry, but in infinite variety, and that this symmetry looks exact, but when observed closely shows small variations.

Because of this geometry it seemed appropriate that the sides of this beaker were flat, and the silver was left smooth and un-engraved to keep the icy feel intended by the pale cool colours of the enamel.'

These four beakers, on the themes of animal, fish, plant and water were originally commissioned with the brief simply as Nature. Together they powerfully now suggest the fragility of the environment today.

Opposite: Detail, 'Lichen' Beaker, 2007

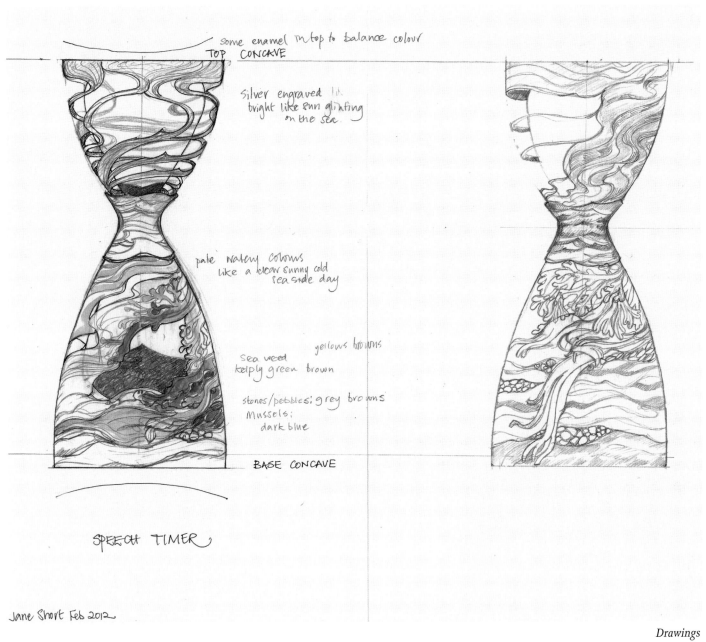

some enamel in top to balance colour

TOP CONCAVE

Silver engraved lit.
bright like sun glinting
on the sea.

pale watery colours
like a clear sunny cold
sea side day

yellows browns
Sea weed
kelply green brown

stones/pebbles: grey browns
Mussels:
dark blue

BASE CONCAVE

SPEECH TIMER

Jane Short Feb 2012

Drawings

SPEECH TIMER, 2014

*Hour glass body made in spun sections,
champlevé enamel, glass and Cornish sand.
Silver made by Clive Burr; designed, hand-
engraved and enamelled by Jane Short.
Commission*
Marks: Jane Short, London
Height 18.6cm · width 8cm

Hourglass form with the base slightly
wider than the top. Engraved and
enamelled with depictions of the
landscape of Cornish beaches, rock
pools, sea and sand. Seaweeds of various
kinds swirl into flowing water patterns,
mussels cram into rock crevices, and a
mackerel shoal swims along the base of
the timer, all executed in the sharp clear
colours of the Cornish coast.

Commissioned to commemorate the
year of office of Mr Michael Galsworthy
as Prime Warden of the Goldsmiths'
Company 2010–2011 for use at Livery
Dinners at Goldsmiths' Hall. The design
brief was to evoke Mr Galsworthy's
Cornish home 'Trewithen', suggesting
the landscape of beaches, marrying the
trickling of sand in the timer with this
Cornish theme.

The timer runs for seven minutes
and the sand is viewed through the
top of the piece where it can be seen
disappearing down into the rock pool
below. The inscription on the top
reads 'Michael Galsworthy Prime
Warden 2010–2011' and was engraved by
Sam James.

Detail of Colour Junction

'COLOUR JUNCTION', 2015

The underlying silver of the enamelled dish carved and engraved in a similar way to that used under basse-taille enamel, but here the enamels laid over have been allowed to follow and emphasise that carved surface. Finely ground and wet process enamels applied for the final firings of the enamel to create heavily textured areas, adding an extra dimension to the piece.

Designed, hand engraved and enamelled by Jane Short. Silver made by Clive Burr Commission

Marks: Jane Short, London

Height 10cm · length 53cm · width 21cm

Referencing the qualities of mark making used in painting and drawing, with particular interest in the work of Kandinsky, 'Colour Junction' is a meeting of colour, form, and surface texture , using rich enamel colour contrasts, abstract engraving and carving on silver to create a dynamic sculptural but functional centrepiece.

'I have always found enamel to have a quality of colour that allows such a breadth of expression; it can be lyrical and sweet, poetic, subdued, rich, solid, subtle – in this piece I was aiming for a dynamic interplay of colour, shape, pattern and texture, both exhilarating and edgy, to invoke a response in the viewer similar to that which I have to certain colour combinations of colour and texture, whatever the medium. Here I have had the chance to explore enamel in an expressive and painterly way, over a form that changes greatly depending on its viewing point.'

Jane Short, 2015

'Your brain did not evolve to see absolutes. Light coming from any particular surface is constantly changing. The way the brain sees colour is by looking for relationships, whether local or overall. The brain is never seeing what is there; interpretation of the world is not fixed; context plays its part as well as the individual's emotional state when witnessing colour.'

Dr Beau Lotto, Neuroscientist, University College, London, 2015

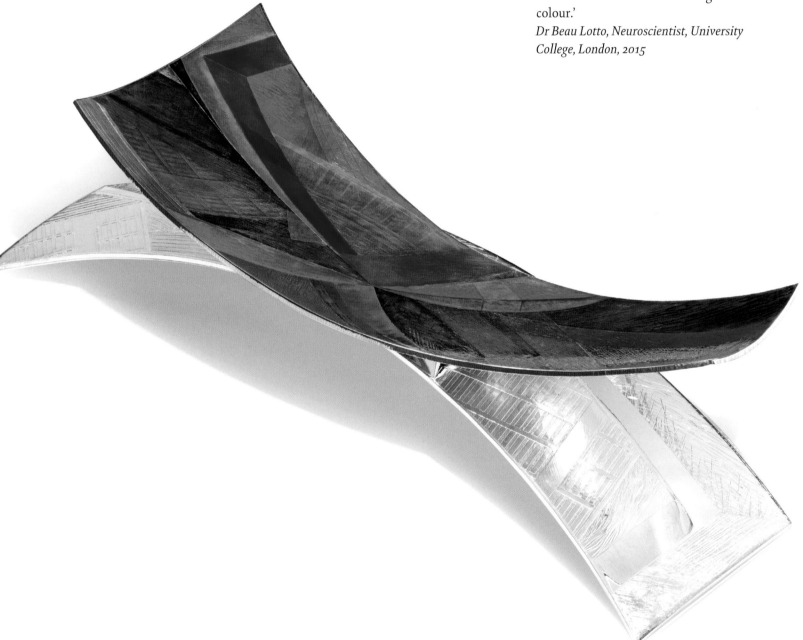

MARY ANN SIMMONS

'Silver is a material that has captivated me for over 20 years, not only for its beauty but its unique properties. The art of contemporary box making is central to my work, with its clean lines and geometry, demanding precision and expert technique.

This exploration of complex form does not end at the exterior. The interior is of equal importance and often provides the canvas for creating highly personalised objects unique to the client; handwritten letters, children's drawings and family signatures all combine with the silver piece to create heirlooms of the future.'

Born Canada, 1959. Graduate of Sir John Cass Faculty, London Metropolitan University, 1997. Master's degree, Royal College of Art, 2000.

Mary Ann Simmons uses traditional silversmithing skills of scoring and folding for box making, hammering, forming, construction, soldering and etching to explore simple and complex forms. Her studio workshop is in Swansea, Wales.

Public Collections include:
2001 'Imminent Change' Art Medal, The British Museum, London;
2003 'The Fourth Service' 1939-45 Art Medal, The British Museum, London.

Selected Commissions include:
2003 'The Fourth Service', British Art Medals Society;
2003 Box, HM King Constantine of Greece;
2007 'Silver Rim', Past Overseers Society of St Margaret & St John the Evangelist, Westminster;
2008/9 '2 Temple Place', Richard Hoare, C. Hoare & Co. (collaboration with Vicki Ambery-Smith);
2009/10 'Bowls with College Crest', The Sir Joseph Larmor Plate, St John's College, Cambridge;

2012 'Tercentenary', Past Overseers Society of St Margaret & St John the Evangelist, Westminster;
2014 'Silver Horn Box Plinth', Past Overseers Society of St Margaret & St John the Evangelist, Westminster.

THREE 'PERSPECTIVE' BOXES, 2005

Britannia silver, constructed from sheet.
Purchase
Mark: Mary Ann Simmons, London
Large: height 13.4cm · width 10.9cm
Small A: height 9.2cm · width 8.3cm
Small B: height 9.2cm · width 8.2cm

Open top 'business card' boxes with angled sides giving a perspective appearance for those who like fiddling with objects on their desk.

'INDULGENCE PLATTER', 2007

Britannia silver, sunken oval form.
Purchase
Marks: Mary Ann Simmons, London
Height 2.5cm · width 35.5cm

For the maker it's in the forming and finishing of the silver, for the server, in the setting out of food on the platter. The moment of indulgence is marked by the maker in the 'bites' taken out of the dish, for the person serving, in the arranging and offering of food and, for the person partaking, in the viewing and tasting.

SMALL, MEDIUM AND LARGE 'PANEL' VESSELS, 2011

Forming and decorative techniques used, cutting, hammering, forming, filing, fitting and soldering. Matt finish.
Purchase
Marks: Mary Ann Simmons, London
Small: height 9.3cm · width 7.5cm
Medium: height 10.5cm · width 9.5cm
Large: height 13cm · width 12cm

'Panel' Vessels, so called because the three vessels are constructed from curved and shaped panels of silver. By shaping, filing and careful fitting the once simple flat plates are assembled into a 3D object reminiscent of a flower pod and offering surprising and varied perspectives.

HIROSHI SUZUKI

'The Japanese are good at surface texture and line, not so good at form. Coming to England I found a way of seeing Japan from the outside.'

Hiroshi does not make a plan by drawing. *'If I did, there would be no reason to make the work – I want to enjoy how things develop in making. I think of silver being a soft living thing. I talk to the material as if it were a person.'*

Born Japan, 1961. Master's degree, Musashino Art University, Tokyo, 1988. Graduate of Camberwell College of Art, London, 1997. Master's degree, Royal College of Art, 1999. Senior Fellow, Bishopsland Educational Trust. Currently Professor of Metalwork and Jewellery at Musashino Art University.

Hiroshi Suzuki specialises in hammering, raising and chasing to create decorative vessels which are fluent expression of nature. Hiroshi's studio workshops are in Tokyo and London.

Public Collections include:
1997 'Figure S' (B-2) and 'L&S-4', Shipley Art Gallery, Gateshead;

1997 'Dual-Rivulet 2', Cheongju National Museum, Cheongju, South Korea;
1999 'Aqua-Poesy IV' Vase, The P&O Makower Trust donated to the Victoria and Albert Museum, London, for their permanent collection;
2001 'Figure D' (Konoe 2), and 'Komame 2', Birmingham Museum and Art Gallery;
2002 'Aqua-Poesy VII', Crafts Council, London;
2004 'Aqua-Poesy VII', Sainsbury Centre for Visual Arts, Norwich;
2004 'Aqua-Poesy VI' (ver.2id), Aberdeen Art Gallery & Museum;
2004 'Aqua-Poesy VII', Ulster Museum, Belfast;
2004 'Tou-la II', National Museums Scotland, Edinburgh;
2005 'Aqua-Poesy XI', National Museums Liverpool, Merseyside;
2005 'M-Fire II', National Museum Wales, Cardiff;
2005 'Dual-Rivulet 7' (ver.3), Bristol City Museum & Art Gallery;
2005 'Aqua-Poesy IX', Musée Mandet, Riom, France;
2005 'M-Fire I', Art Gallery of South Australia, Adelaide, Australia;
2006 'M-Fire I', The Fitzwilliam Museum, Cambridge;
2006 'Dual-Rivulet 8' (ver.3), National Museums Scotland, Edinburgh;
2006 'Dual-Rivulet 7' (ver.4), Museum of Arts and Design, New York, USA;
2006 'Aqua-Poesy V' (ver.6), The Museum of Fine Arts, Houston, Texas, USA;
2007 'M-Fire Dom' Beaker, The Metropolitan Museum of Art, New York, USA;
2008 'Aqua-Poesy II', Millennium Gallery, Museums Sheffield;

2008 'M-Fire I', Museum für Kunst und Gewerbe, Hamburg, Germany;
2010 'Earth I', Ashmolean Museum, Oxford.

Selected Commissions include:
2000 'Dual-Rivulet 3', New College, Oxford;
2004 'Aqua-Poesy VI', and 'Aqua-Poesy VI' (Ver.2), The Worshipful Company of Clothworkers, London;
2006 'Millennium Punch Bowls', The Sheffield Assay Office;
2006 Set of Candlesticks, His Grace the Duke of Devonshire;
2006 'Dual-Rivulet 7', The Worshipful Company of Grocers, London;
2007 'M-Fire VI', The Worshipful Company of Salters, London.

There is no tradition of large pieces of silver in Japan. For years Hiroshi concentrated on one symmetrical form. The vase became his canvas. Each piece has a dynamic presence with Suzuki's poetry defining the work. Working within the Japanese tradition of the spirituality of natural elements such as wind and water, Suzuki makes these abstractions accessible to Western eyes through his sculptural approach to his vessels. In Zen philosophy the five senses are the same as in Western thought with the exception of touch. Feeling is not transmitted through the fingertips alone but through the whole body. For Suzuki the making process is an intensely physical one but one in which the mind is also constantly active. He applies himself to his material like a force of nature. The integrity of his single technique of hammering transmits powerfully through his work without the viewer necessarily being aware of the process. Instead the viewer is intensely aware of the physical presence of Suzuki's pieces and their spiritual connection to nature.

'AQUA-POESY V' VASE, 2001

Fine Silver, hand–raised without the use of a conventional stake. Horizontal fluting 'hammered on-air'. Body has concave fluting running around the outside and a planished matt finish.
Purchase
Marks: Hiroshi Suzuki, London
Height 30.5cm · diameter 17.5cm

The vase takes on the pliability of clay to form a vessel which echoes fluent expressions found in nature.

'DUAL-RIVULET VII'
DOUBLE SKINNED BOWL, 2001

*Fine silver (999). Hammer-raised, double-
skinned bowl with shallow concave fluting
running around the outside of the body.
The outer body matt with a fine-textured
hammer finish, the inside of the bowl bright
planished finish.*
Commission
Marks: Hiroshi Suzuki, London
Height 16.5cm · diameter 29cm

'Thinking through making' guides
Hiroshi Suzuki in creating a new
dynamic tension here between surface
and texture.

'AQUA-POESY VII' VASE, 2003

Britannia silver. Hand-raised, hammered and chased. Body decorated with furrows spiralling from base to neck, troughs between ridges are softly textured and matt white finished. Tops of ridges are bright finished to contrast with matt areas.
Purchase
Marks: Hiroshi Suzuki, London
Height 30.6cm · diameter 18cm

Part of a series of vases exploring the subtleties of fluidity within a form and on a surface to create a work that belongs to a conceptual realm of appreciation, a poetry of water.

Purchased after being exhibited at the 'Creation' exhibition held at Goldsmiths' Hall, 2004.

'AYAWIND II' VASE, 2005

Britannia silver. Hand-raised and hand-chased spiral ridges rising up the body with horizontal ridges chased into the troughs between rising ridges.
Purchase
Marks: Hiroshi Suzuki, London
Height 34.5cm · width 21.0cm

Hiroshi Suzuki now has work in numerous national and international museums and private collections. Short-listed for the Jerwood Applied Arts Prize 2005, this vase was purchased from his collection of new work for this exhibition. The vase displays Hiroshi Suzuki's technical ability to give silver vigour and movement to create a work of beauty and originality, evoking wind rustling through leaves, and perhaps a sense of fabric. He leaves it to the imagination.

LUCIAN TAYLOR

'A recurring theme in my work has been a questioning of the meaning of choosing silver as a medium in which to produce functional items. Where lies the value of a work in silver – in material, art or craft? I am investigating the beauty and ugliness I have found in excess. This has been distilled into an exploration of hollow forms made from metal membranes.'

Born 1967. Graduate of Brighton Polytechnic 1989. Master's degree, Royal College of Art, 1992.

Lucian Taylor has developed an experimental approach to silversmithing techniques, concentrating on ground-breaking processes that explore the possibilities of viewing metal as a membrane. He embraces digital technologies both to design and to produce his work. His studio workshop is in Oxford.

Public Collections include:
1996 Fish Server, The Rabinovitch Collection at the Victoria and Albert Museum, London;

2000 Handled Pepper and Salt, Birmingham Museum and Art Gallery;
2000 Millennium Canteen, Millennium Gallery, Museums Sheffield;
2004 Dish, Hove Museum and Art Gallery.

Selected Commissions include:
2001 115 Silver Pens and Pen Stands, commemorating the completion of the Citigroup and HSBC buildings in Canary Wharf;
2003 Pair of Candelabra, Wadham College, Oxford.

The Goldsmiths' Company Modern Silver Collection (not included in the exhibition):
1995 Water Jug.

FLASK, 2005

Made in seven panels with raised seams, sections flame-welded together, the whole object then inflated under high pressure. Matt finish with light oxidisation.
Purchase
Marks: Lucian Taylor, London
Height 25cm · diameter 15cm

'Superabundant' is a body of work which grew out of experiments exploring the theme of silver and other metals as a membrane.

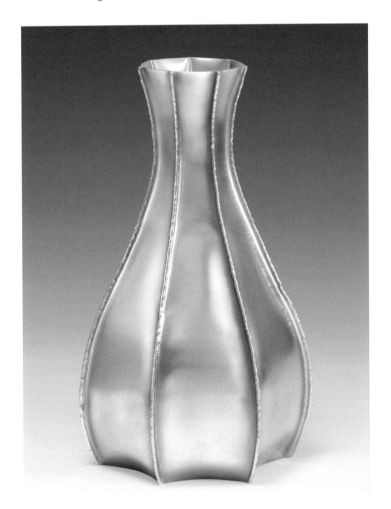

'DOUBLE SPHERE' MESH BOWL, 2009

Hand moulded over a steel former using 930 Argentium silver wire.
Purchase
Marks: Lucian Taylor, London
Height 23cm · diameter 29cm

The bowl is part of an exploration of alternative methods of creating innovative hollow ware of a sphere within a sphere. The virtual perfect precision of mesh of a computer aided designed object is recreated here by the use of traditional hand skills, hand-soldering in particular, creating an object which reflects its incongruous duality. This odd duality is not only that it originated as a computer design, and then has been hand-made, but also that it is a double sphere. For what function? To display and hold delicious chocolates perhaps.

'Double Sphere' Mesh Bowl was purchased from 'Origin' exhibition, London, 2009.

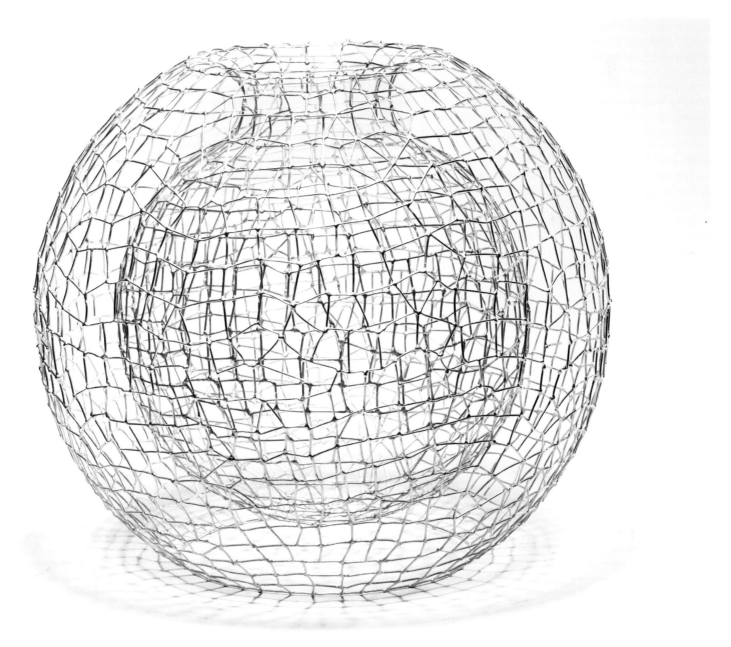

SIMONE TEN HOMPEL

'Every artistic object refers to its maker's existence; it's a trace that indicates: Someone was here and left something behind. Traces of manipulation on its surface – in this case traces on the metal which are at the same time the maker's signature.'

Born Germany, 1960. Diploma Fachhochschule, Dusseldorf, 1985. Master's Degree the Royal College of Art, 1989.Winner of the Jerwood Prize for Metalwork in 2005. Winner, State of Bavaria Award for Applied Art in 2012. Fellow and Current Senior Fellow Bishopsland Educational Trust.

Simone's work highlights that function is of dual importance; if an object is designed to function it must function well, handle well, feel good and fit its purpose. A piece in silver can work through metaphors, such as the function of containment in a vessel, as a body contains a spirit. Her studio workshop is in London.

Public Collections include:
1990 Oil and Vinegar set, P&O Makower Trust, donated to the Victoria and Albert Museum, London;
1993 Cake Slice, The Rabinovitch Collection at the Victoria and Albert Museum, London;
1995 Container, National Museums Scotland, Edinburgh;
1995 'Line Up' Container, the Crafts Council, London;
1997 Bowl, Shipley Art Gallery, Gateshead;
2000 Container, Birmingham Museum and Art Gallery;
2000 Vessel, the Crafts Council, London;
2002 Drinking implement, Shipley Art Gallery, Gateshead;
2003 Containers, 'A Field of Silver, Silver, Silver in a Field', Birmingham Museum and Art Gallery;
2004 'Billy Boy' Container, Aberdeen Museum and Art Gallery;
2005 'Glowing Shadow' Container, Birmingham Museum and Art Gallery;

2005 Five Spoons, The Crafts Council, London;
2008 Container, National Museum Wales, Swansea.

Selected Commissions include:
2000 Millennium Canteen, Millennium Gallery, Museums Sheffield.

The Goldsmiths' Company Modern Silver Collection (not included in the exhibition):
1997 Napkin Ring.

'APHRODITE' DISH, 2004

Domed and counter-domed hammered shallow dish.
Matt finished with pale faceted Indian sapphire
from Jaipur in a platinum setting on rim.
Purchase
Marks: Simone Ten Hompel, London
length 31cm · width 30.2cm

Neither a utilitarian vessel nor jewellery,
this plate intentionally emphasises the
tactile beauty of silver. Purchased after
being exhibited at the 'Creation' exhibition
held at Goldsmiths' Hall, 2004.

HAZEL THORN

'I grew up in a remote part of the Highlands, and have always loved wild places and natural objects. I do not use natural or found materials in my work, but explore intuitively with metal, allowing the essence of such themes to surface indirectly.

My sculptural vessels are therefore an exploration and celebration of experimental metalwork techniques. Combining metals then patinating the resulting object creates the bold patterns and colours in my work. This technical, hands-on side of metalwork is central to my practice. I have been investigating the appeal of irregular or imperfect objects, such as ruined buildings, as I prefer a dilapidated or roughly-constructed aesthetic to one of precise and shining beauty. Observation both of natural materials such as tree bark and disintegrating manmade objects informs my work, appearing in an abstracted way in the patterns and forms I create.'

Born Scotland, 1988. Master's degree in Fine Art and Silversmithing, Edinburgh College of Art, 2014.

Hazel's practice as a silversmith revolves around workshop experimentation. Using both base and precious metals, she constructs sheets whose patterns are created by their method of assembly. Hazel applies a single chemical patina to the whole object, which affects the metals in different ways. This produces contrasting colours which highlight the structure of the sheet. Hazel's studio workshop is in Scotland.

Selected Commissions include:
2011 Goblet, The Incorporation of Goldsmiths, Edinburgh;
2011 Mokume Gane section, The University of The Highlands & Islands Ceremonial Mace, Scotland.

Test pieces

Inspiration

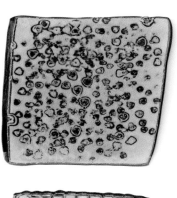

Test pieces

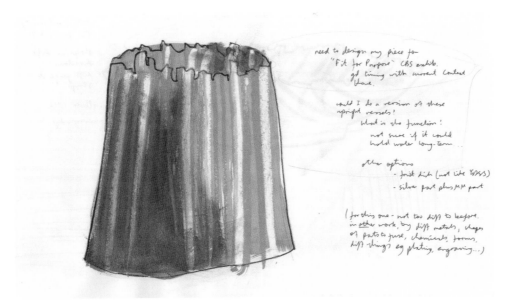

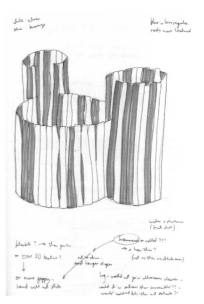

Drawings

'WRAPPED BIRCH' VESSEL, 2011

Sterling silver, gilding metal and solder. Rods of silver and gilding metal are fused and rolled into a flat sheet, which is then formed. After construction is finished, the piece is sanded and placed in ammonia vapour, which has a different reaction with each metal used. Silver remains white, gilding metal turns black, and the areas where these two metals are alloyed patinate to create a turquoise-blue.
Purchase
Marks: Hazel Thorn, Edinburgh
Height 10.8cm · width 8.5cm

This piece stems from Hazel's intensive material research into mixed metals and patination. Her development of experimental constructing and casting processes led to the technique used to create this bold pattern.

In addition to the process-led elements of this design, it is influenced by her upbringing in the Scottish Highlands. An appreciation of the beautiful and sometimes harsh landscape contributed to the natural and irregular and weathered aesthetic in this work, the illusion of an object found in the Scottish wilderness.

This piece was acquired from Hazel when she was still a research student, aged 23, at Edinburgh College of Art, following her presentation before the Modern Collection Committee in 2011, making her the youngest silversmith represented in the Collection then.

ADI TOCH

'The practice of making vessels and containers fascinates me as it enables me to work both with metal and space as materials, redefining borders between inside and outside. Through my work I explore the morphological qualities of vessels and the process of embedding functional objects with spirit. I create contemplative work, communicating through tactile essence.

Some vessels are designed to invite interaction and play – they contain substances like sand or tiny pearls, which can be seen, felt and heard, but not emptied or spilt. The content is shifted as the object is held, making gentle sound and creating illusive patterns. Oil Drizzlers are double-layered pourers with top funnelling to the interior and a tiny spout for drizzling. These vessels suggest a different experience of pouring – guiding the liquid through the tiny spout, they only tease the onlooker that they will spill from top.'

Born Israel, 1979. Graduate Bezalel Art Academy in Jerusalem, 2004. Master's degree, The Cass Faculty of Art, Architecture and Design, London Metropolitan University, 2009. Senior Fellow of the Bishopsland Educational Trust.

Adi uses traditional silversmithing skills of spinning, raising and fabrication, producing vessels with matt finishes as well as patination. Her studio workshop is in London.

Public Collections include:
2008 Bowl, Turnov Museum, Czech Republic;
2012 'Red Sand' Bowl, Crafts Council Collection, London;
2012 'Little Beak' Oil Drizzler, Crafts Council Collection, London;
2012 'Pitom' Spice Holder, The Jewish Museum, New York;
2012 'Reflection' Bowl, Fitzwilliam Museum, Cambridge;
2014 'Slanted' Red Sand Bowl, National Museums Scotland, Edinburgh;
2014 'Wide Open', P&O Makower Trust commission donated to National Museum Wales, Cardiff.

'SOUND' VESSEL, 2009

Britannia silver, 18ct gold solder, steel ball bearings. Spun, raised and fabricated. Double-skinned vessel with an opening. Trapped within the bowl are small ball bearings producing sound.
Purchase
Marks: Adi Toch, London
Height 6.8cm · diameter 9cm

The series of tactile vessels invites the observer to touch, play and discover unexpected sounds and motion. Turning the vessels around triggers both a compelling sound and a mesmerizing fluidity of the particles held inside which cannot fall out due to the special structure. It provides the viewer with a few moments of contemplation.

'RED SAND' BOWL, 2009

Britannia silver, red beads. Spun, top part
raised. Trapped within the bowl are tiny red
beads the size of sand grains.
Purchase
Marks: Adi Toch, London
Height 5cm · diameter 8.2cm

The piece raises questions to the viewer
about containment and discovery.

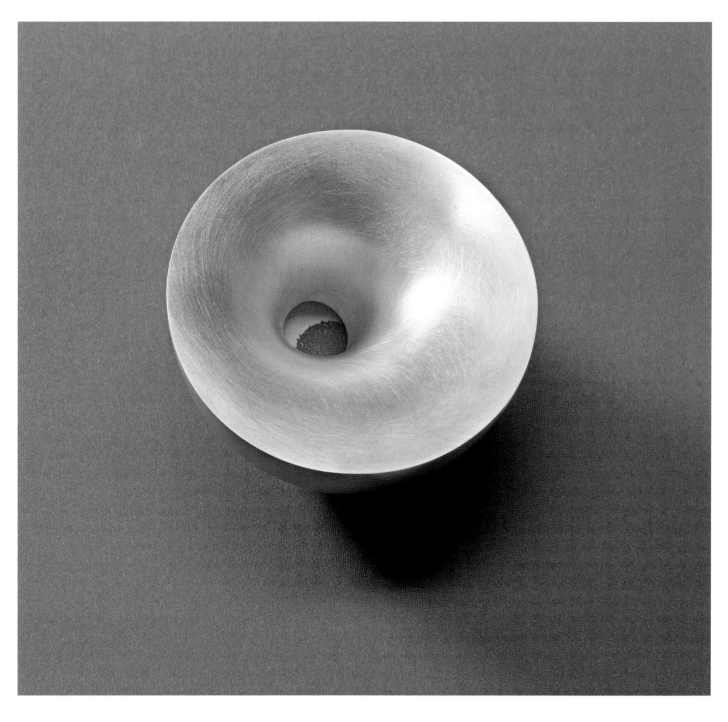

'TIPA' OIL DRIZZLER, 2010

Britannia silver. Spun, raised and fabricated.
Double skinned jug.
Purchase
Marks: Adi Toch, London
Height 7.1cm · diameter 8.5cm

'Oil Drizzlers' are a series of jugs which
are designed in a way that oil will drizzle
only from the little spout. The shapes
are inspired by enchained clay scrolls
discovered near the Dead Sea.

    'Tipa' Oil Drizzler was purchased from
Goldsmiths' Fair, 2010.

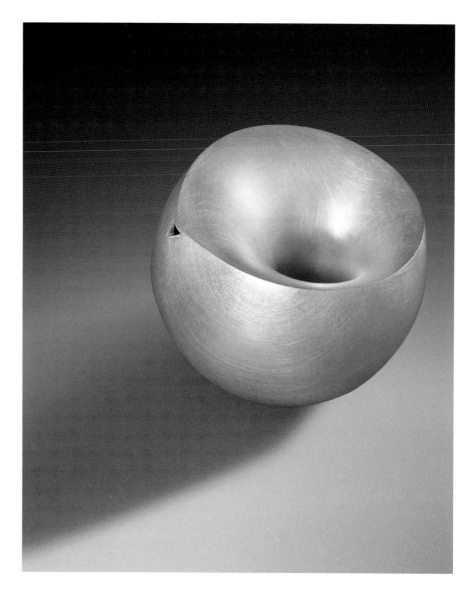

'PINCH OF SALT BOWL', 2010

Gold plated Britannia silver. Hand-raised and
formed. Double skinned bowl, gilt overall.
Commission
Marks: Adi Toch, London
Height 6.2cm · diameter 12.7cm

The measurement bowl designed in
such a way that just one pinch of salt at
a time should be accessible through the
opening. The salt will not spill out if the
bowl is tipped over.

KEITH TYSSEN

'A design should be apt, well-conceived and realised through a well-managed combination of invention, good technique, material, construction and thoughtful finish. These things together are essential ingredients for arriving at a fine quality product, and a good design is all of that. I prefer design that makes a bold visual statement, but calmly (mostly) and well-tempered enough to equip an object with a reassuring presence, enabling it to stand alone or to harmonise within its setting. For me, this forms a major part of the appeal of any good design, no matter its market value or social status.'

Born 1934. Master's degree, Royal College of Art, 1960.

Keith Tyssen brings a highly disciplined 'eye' of a designer silversmith to his range of materials which he forms into domestic silver using both mechanical and hand skills. His studio workshop is in Sheffield.

Selected Commissions from a list of over 52 commissions 1958–2009 include:
1958/9 Bishop's Morse and a Verger's Wand, Guildford Cathedral;
1959 Ceremonial Mace, The Furniture Makers' Guild;
1965/66 Pair of Two 15-light Candelabrum, Exeter University (gift of the Goldsmiths' Company);
1967 Gilded Cross suspended above the Altar in the Chapel of Churchill College, Cambridge (gift of the Goldsmiths' Company);
1967 OSRAM Motor Racing Trophy, BARC Saloon Car Race Competition;
1968 Chalice and Paten for Catholic Communion at Heathrow Airport Chapel, (gift of the Goldsmiths' Company);
1969 Poseybowl, The Worshipful Company of Armourers and Brasiers, London;
1970 Ceremonial Mace, UK Parliamentary 'Independence Gift' to the Parliament of Mauritius;
1970 Pair of Wall Sconces, The Worshipful Company of Dyers;
1973 Pair of Four-light Candelabra, The Worshipful Company of Plumbers, commissioned by Lord Farringdon;
1973 An Edition of 200 Hall Marked Silver Railway Tickets for the North Yorkshire Moors Historical Railway Trust, celebrating the re-opening of steam train services on the line from Grosmont to Pickering;
1975 Table Centrepiece, Commissioned by HM Government as the Independence Gift to the people of the Bahamas Islands;
1976 Champagne Mug, Lady Elizabeth Cavendish for Sir John Betjeman on his 70th Birthday;
1983 Casket, the retiring Lord Mayor of Sheffield, commissioned by Sheffield City Council;
1988 Two Candlesticks, an Altar Cross and a Processional Cross, The Holy Trinity Church, Millhouses, Sheffield;
1994 Ceremonial Mace, Humberside University, Lincoln;
2000 Six Pieces for the 'Sefer Torah' Sheffield Jewish Congregation and Centre (SJCC);
1999/2000   The Millennium Punchbowl; Commissioned by Sheffield's Assay Master for permanent display in the Millennium Gallery, Museums Sheffield. This large piece represents a collaborative design making a triumph for: Alex Brogden, Chris Knight, Brett Payne and Keith Tyssen;

The Goldsmiths' Company Modern Silver Collection (not included in the exhibition):
1964 Paper weight;
1966 Topham Six-Light Candelabrum;
1967 Paper weight.

BOWL, 2009

Double-skinned bowl with partial
oxidised finish.
Purchase
Marks: Keith Tyssen, Sheffield
Height 6.1cm · diameter 17.5cm

The darker tones of the oxidised silver
give a dramatic effect to this simple
form for domestic use.

MAX WARREN

'I have always loved to make things. I first found an affinity with metal whilst at Brighton University when I was studying 3D craft and design. In my final year I became absorbed by hand raising and forging techniques. I enjoyed the direct contact with my material and the counter-intuitive idea that metal could be moved like clay. As I became more engaged with the field of silversmithing, my focus developed around reinterpreting traditional craft techniques to convey contemporary ideas. I am inspired by digital manufacturing processes and aesthetics but produce objects entirely by hand, using ancient craft techniques. The aim is to create works that resonate at once with an historical context and with contemporary life. Precious material in a digital age.'

Born 1982. Graduated from University of Brighton, 2006. Bishopsland Fellow 2006–2007. Master's degree, Royal College of Art, 2009. Current Senior Fellow of the Bishopsland Trust. Senior Lecturer, BA Jewellery Design, Central Saint Martins, UAL, London. Max's studio workshop is in London.

Public Collections include:
2007 Spheric Vessel, Fitzwilliam Museum, Cambridge;
2010 Candlestick, P&O Makower Trust commission donated to the Victoria and Albert Museum, London.

Selected Commissions include:
2009 Silver Maker Arm Braker, Royal College of Art, London;
2010 Vase, The Pearson Collection, London.

'ORNAMENT 1' PLATE, 2012

Hammer-formed, hand-engraved.
Purchase
Marks: Max Warren, London
Diameter 20cm

The engraved imagery is derived from a quote by Franz Sales Meyer, from his 1888 HANDBOOK OF ORNAMENT; 'The term "ORNAMENT" in its limited sense, includes such of the elements of Decoration as are adapted, or developed, from Natural Foliage ... i.e. possessing stems, leaves, flowers &c. ...' This was used in a very direct way as a recipe for creating ornament on this plate.

YUSUKE YAMAMOTO

'I'm fascinated with faces. Behaviour of water and cloud, petals, and grains of trees ... this eye-catching part inspires the whole picture. The face itself begins the story. I think that there could be a face in every natural matter. My working process starts from where to look for such a face. And I develop the motif which touches my heart. I shape metal with hammering and chasing. Each stroke marks a story of its expression, atmosphere, and emotion. Between my work and a receiver, a new story is completed there. Diversity of this face, be it animal, human or abstract is the factor that attracts me, and it is the key to my work.'

Born Japan, 1979. Graduated from Musashino Art University, Tokyo, 2004. Worked at Musashino Art University as a Research associate under Hiroshi Suzuki. Academic Researcher Glasgow School of Art, 2012. Visiting lecturer at Glasgow School of Art 2014. Guest Fellow of the Bishopsland Educational Trust.

Yusuke uses traditional silversmithing skills of hammering and chasing. His studio workshop is in Glasgow.

Selected Commissions include:
2015 Finger Bowl, New College, Oxford.

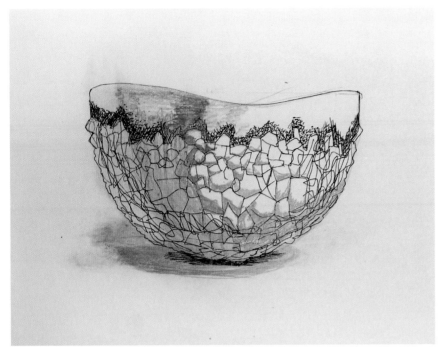
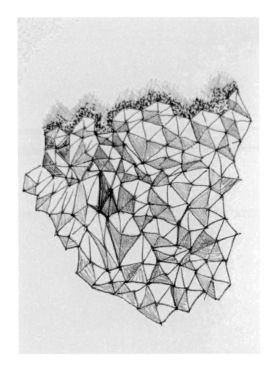

Drawings

'SWEET SQUAMA' BOWL, 2015

*Hand-raised and chased using
handmade punches.*
Commission
Marks: Yusuke Yamamoto, Edinburgh
Height 15cm · width 23cm

Commissioned following a similar bowl exhibited at Goldsmiths' Fair, 2014. Yusuke bases this larger bowl on the image of Durian fruit and a reptile's scales.

Hallmark punches

HALLMARKING

The word 'hallmark' literally means mark of Goldsmiths' Hall. Craftsmen were required by ordinance in the late 15th century to bring their gold and silver wares to the Hall to be assayed and then stamped with the mark set down by statute. The London Assay Office was housed in Goldsmiths' Hall in 1478. Still there today, it is the oldest hallmarking authority in the United Kingdom, and continues hallmarking under Act of Parliament. On average over 3 million articles of silver, gold, platinum and palladium are assayed each year. X-Ray Fluorescence Analysis is now the most widely used method to ascertain silver quality, as opposed to the former method of volumetric titration. The age-old touchstone method is still used for a quick indication of precious metal content by expert staff.

Once assayed, and found to be up to the legal standard required, each silver piece will be marked with several hallmarks.

A GUIDE TO HALLMARKS

 Sponsor's Mark (indicating the maker or sponsor of the article). Here for Hector Miller.

 The Standard Mark, a voluntary mark, here indicating sterling silver.

 The Metal Purity Mark (indicating the fineness of the article). Here Sterling Standard silver (92.5% purity of silver, 7.5% alloy).

 The Assay Office Mark or Town Mark (indicating the particular Assay Office at which the article was tested and marked). Here the leopard's head for the London Assay Office.

 The Date Letter, a voluntary mark (indicating the year the article was marked). Here 'P' for 2014. The design of the date letter changes once the cycle of the alphabet has been exhausted.

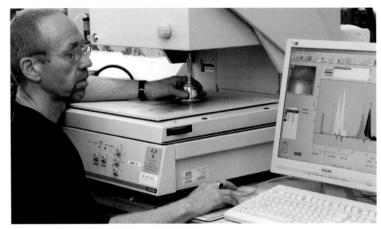

X-Ray Fluorescence Analysis

Use of Touchstone

Hand marking at the London Assay Office.

THE UK ASSAY OFFICES

 LONDON    BIRMINGHAM

 SHEFFIELD   EDINBURGH

London Assay Office was established at Goldsmiths' Hall in 1478.

There are three other assay offices in the United Kingdom:

The oldest of the three is in Edinburgh, regulated by the
Incorporation of Goldsmiths there, which has existed since the 1490s.

Birmingham Assay Office was established by Act of Parliament
in 1773

Sheffield Assay Office was established by Act of Parliament in 1773.

All four assay offices unified the date letter system of rotation.
The date letter changes in alphabetical order each year. Date letter 'q'
is for 2015.

The design of the date letter also changes once the cycle of the
alphabet has been exhausted; since 1975 all four assay offices have
used the same design for each new cycle of the alphabet date letter.
It remains a voluntary mark, but all silversmiths represented in the
Company's Modern Collection request a date letter hallmark to
identify the date of their work.

DIRECTORY OF SPONSOR'S MARKS

Sponsor's marks of the silversmiths represented in *The Silversmith's Art: Made in Britain Today* exhibition

APPLEBY, Malcolm, b.1946 (Liveryman)

BROGDEN, Alex, b.1954 (Liveryman)

BURR, Clive, b.1953 (Liveryman)

BURTON, Jocelyn, b.1946 (Freeman)

CHAMBERLAIN, Julie, b.1958 (Freeman)

CHRISTENSEN, Ane, b.1972 (Freeman)

CLARKE, David, b.1967

COATES, Kevin, b.1950 (Liveryman)

CONWAY, Rosamond, b.1951 (Freeman)

CORK, Angela, b.1973 (Freeman)

DE QUIN, Rebecca, b.1958 (Freeman)

DEVLIN, Stuart, b.1931 (Liveryman, Former Assistant, Prime Warden 1996–1997)

DICK, Lexi, b.1951 (Liveryman)

DORPH-JENSEN, Sidsel, b.1973 (Associate)

EKUBIA, Ndidi, b.1973 (Freeman)

FOX, Richard, b.1954 (Assistant)

GREY, Kevin, b.1967

HANID, Miriam, b.1986

HIGSON, Rauni, b.1970 (Freeman)

HINTON, Kathryn, b.1981

HOPE, Adrian, b.1953 (Freeman)

JUNG, Kyosun, b.1984

KAPRALOVA, Petya, b.1986

KELLY, Rod, b.1956 (Liveryman)

KNIGHT, Christopher, b.1964 (Freeman)

LEE, William (Sang-Hyeob), b.1974

LIU, Nan Nan, b.1982

LLOYD, Michael, b.1950 (Freeman)

LORD, Esther, b.1981

LORENZ, Anna, b.1967

LOWE, Olivia, b.1981

LOYEN, Frances, b.1951 (Freeman)

MACDONALD, Grant, b.1947 (Assistant, Prime Warden 2008–2009)

MCCAIG, Grant, b.1974

MCCALLUM, Alistair, b.1953 (Freeman)

MCDONALD, Sheila, b.1958 (Freeman)

MCFADYEN, Angus, b.1962 (Freeman)

MEETEN, Wayne, b.1961 (Freeman)

MILLER, Hector, b.1945 (Assistant, Prime Warden 2011–2012)

MORI, Junko, b.1974 (Freeman)

NGUYEN, Theresa, b.1985 (Freeman)

O'DUBHGHAILL, Cóilín, b.1974

O'NEILL, Shannon, b.1971

OTTEWILL, Steven, b.1968 (Freeman)

Padgham & Putland
PADGHAM, Carl, b.1963 (Freeman)
PUTLAND, Andrew, b.1963 (Freeman)

PERRY, Christopher, b.1974

PORRITT, Don, b.1933

RAMSAY, Alexandra, b.1973 (Freeman)

RANSOM, Clare, b.1964

RAPHAEL, Alexandra, b.1945

RAWNSLEY, Pamela, 1952 – 2014. (Freeman)

RICH, Fred, b.1954. (Liveryman)

ROBERTSON, Linda, b.1965

ROWE, Michael, b. 1948 (Freeman)

RUSSELL, Toby, b.1963 (Freeman)

SHORT, Jane, b.1954 (Liveryman)

SIMMONS, Mary Ann, b.1959 (Freeman)

SUZUKI, Hiroshi, b.1961 (Associate)

TAYLOR, Lucian, b. 1967 (Freeman)

TEN HOMPEL, Simone, b. 1960

THORN, Hazel, b. 1988

TOCH, Adi, b.1979

TYSSEN, Keith, b.1934 (Liveryman)

WARREN, Max, b.1982

YAMAMOTO, Yusuke, b. 1979

Drawing by Michael Lloyd

'The pencil is a thinking tool.
A sketchbook is a visual memory.'
ROSEMARY RANSOME WALLIS

Inside cover key:

Enamelling	*Patination*	*Modelling*
Detail from *Wafer Box* by Rosamond Conway	Detail from *Wrapped Birch Vessel* by Hazel Thorn	Detail from *Salt* by Lexi Dick
Detail from *Lichen Beaker* by Jane Short	Detail from *Mokume Gane Vase* by Alistair McCallum	Detail from *Charter Bell* by Kevin Coates
Detail from *Shetland Bird Vase* by Sheila McDonald	Detail from *Shakudo Bowl* by Cóilín O'Dubhghaill	Detail from *Millennium Dish* by Stuart Devlin